A-Z AYLESBURY

CONTEN

REFERENCE

A Road	A41	Car Park (selected)	P
B Road	B4009	Church or Chapel	†
Dual Carriageway		Fire Station	■
One-way Street		Hospital	H
Traffic flow on A Roads is also indicated by a heavy line on the driver's left.		House Numbers A & B Roads only	15 3
Restricted Access		Information Centre	i
Pedestrianized Road		National Grid Reference	480
Track / Footpath		Police Station	▲
Residential Walkway		Post Office	★
Cycleway (selected)		Toilet:	
		without facilities for the Disabled	▽
		with facilities for the Disabled	▽
Railway	Heritage Station / Tunnel / Station / Level Crossing	Viewpoint	业
Built-up Area	GREBE CL	Educational Establishment	⌐
		Hospital or Hospice	⌐
Local Authority Boundary	— · — · —	Industrial Building	⌐
		Leisure or Recreational Facility	⌐
Posttown Boundary	————	Place of Interest	⌐
Postcode Boundary (within Posttown)	————	Public Building	⌐
Map Continuation	12	Shopping Centre or Market	⌐
		Other Selected Buildings	⌐

SCALE: 1:15,840   4 inches (10.16 cm) to 1 mile,   6.31 cm to 1 kilometre

0	¼	½	¾	1 Mile
0	250	500	750	1 Kilometre

Copyright of Geographers' A-Z Map Company Limited

Head Office :
Fairfield Road, Borough Green, Sevenoaks, Kent TN15 8PP
Telephone: 01732 781000 (Enquiries & Trade Sales)
01732 783422 (Retail Sales)
www.a-zmaps.co.uk

Copyright © Geographers' A-Z Map Co. Ltd.

Waddesdon

A41

B4011

4

Stone

Upton

A418

Inset
Page 16

8

9

10

Chearsley

Cuddington

Dinton

Haddenham

Ford

Long
Crendon

16

A418

17

18

Kingsey

A4129

River Thame

A418

THAME

24

25

26

A329

Longwick

7

A40

B4445

Pitch
Green

B4012

Tetsworth

Henton

32

Bledlow

M40

30

31

Chinnor

B4009

A40

Lewknor

6

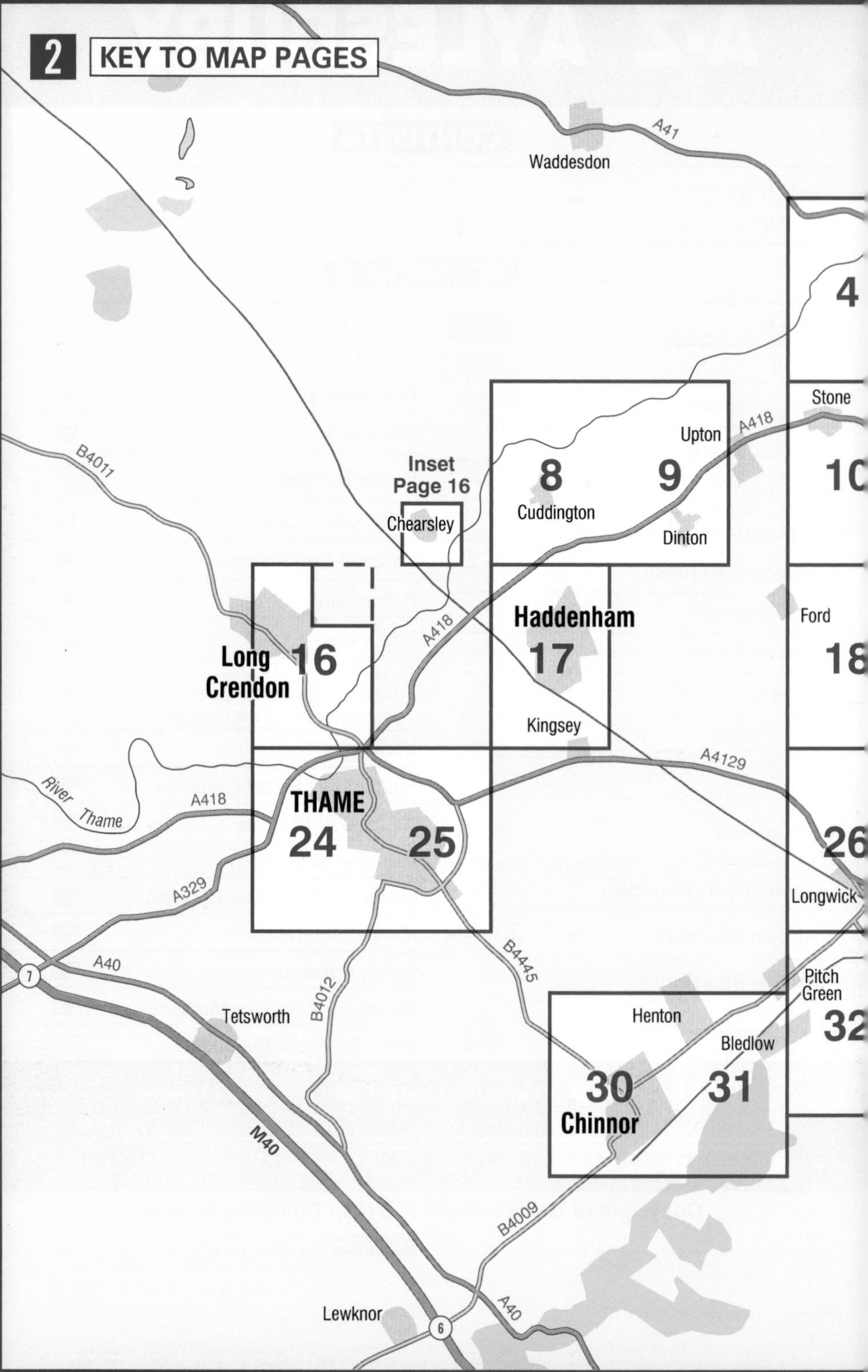

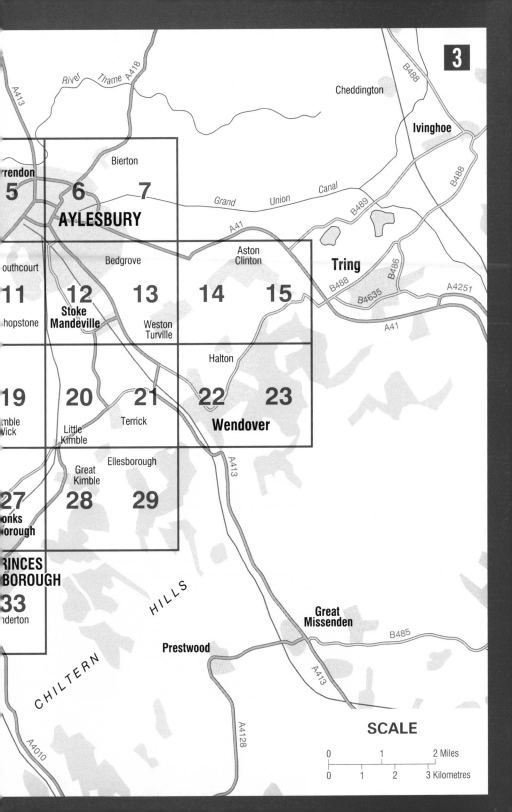

3

Cheddington

Ivinghoe

B488

B488

River Thame A418

A413

rendon

5 **6** **7**

AYLESBURY

Bierton

Grand Union Canal

B489

B488

B486

A4251

outhcourt

Bedgrove

Aston Clinton

Tring

11 **12** **13** **14** **15**

Stoke Mandeville

hopstone

Weston Turville

A41

B488

B4635

A41

Halton

19 **20** **21** **22** **23**

mble Vick

Wendover

Terrick

Little Kimble

Ellesborough

A413

Great Kimble

27 **28** **29**

onks orough

RINCES BOROUGH

33

nderton

CHILTERN

HILLS

Great Missenden

B485

Prestwood

A413

A4010

A4128

SCALE

| 0 | | 1 | | 2 Miles |

| 0 | 1 | 2 | 3 Kilometres |

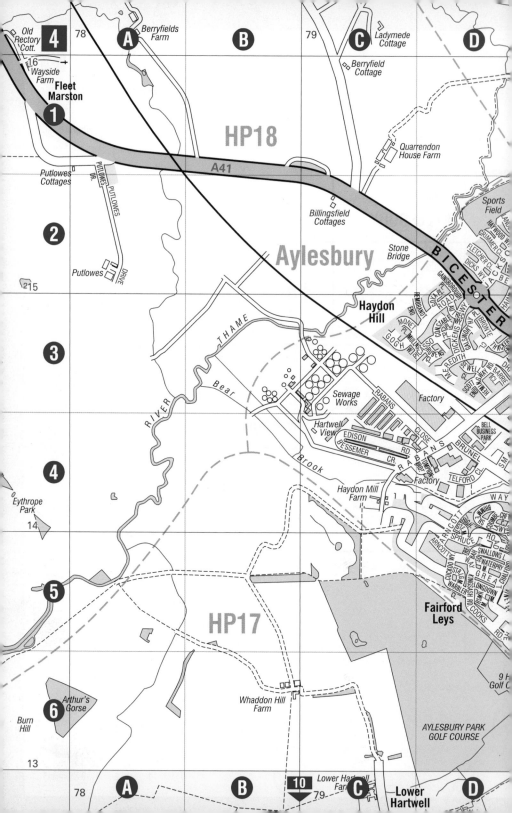

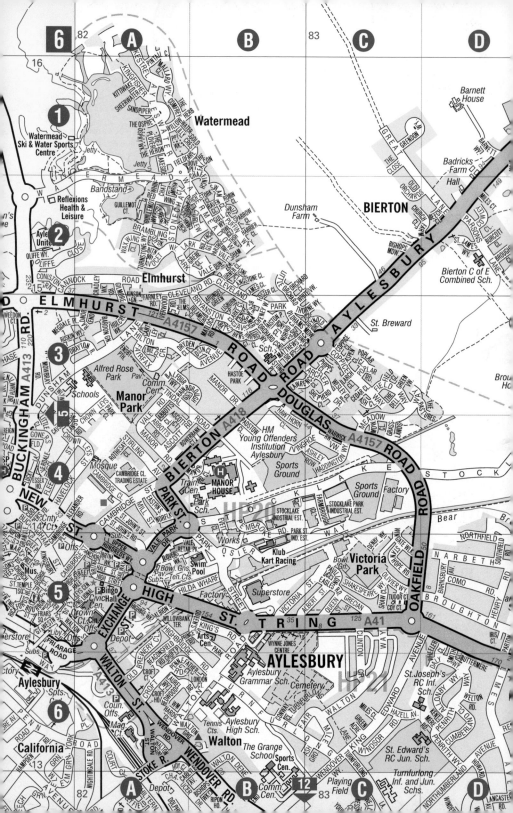

E **F** **G** **H** **7**

16

Grove Farm

ROWSHAM RD

GROVE RD

PECKS FARM

THE FIRS CT.

A418

200

231

HULCOTT

GIB LANE

Club House

Driving Range

LANE

Greenacres 485

New Covert 86

AYLESBURY GOLF COURSE

1

BURCOTT

Bierton Sports Centre

Pav.

Rec Grd

Ten. Cts.

Burcott

MARSHALLS LEA

BROUGHTON LA.

2

215

Burcott Lodge Farm

...lesbury

...TON ...NG

HP22

3

BROUGHTON

Fishery

Grand Union Canal

(Aylesbury Arm)

4

14

P

Amberley

Brook Farm

IVY LA.

Broughton

Girdlers Farm

Oak Farm Rare Breeds Park

Manor Farm

Old Manor Farm

5

Weir

CONNAUGHT RD

RICHMOND

HERON CL.

AVENUE

323

R O A D

242

AYLESBURY HOS.

QUEENS

Bedgrove Brook

THE PADDOCK

HEDGE

GRASS WAYS

NEW MEADOW

MEAD

BEAUFORT CL.

WELBECK

Westend

Ditch

Weston Mead Farm

AKEMAN STREET

LANE

ASTON 41 (Roman Road)

A41 CLINTON

Spirit Health & Fitness Club

BURN HAMS FLD.

NEW ROAD

ROAD

6

Depot

13

E **F** **13** **G** **H**

485

Library

72

86

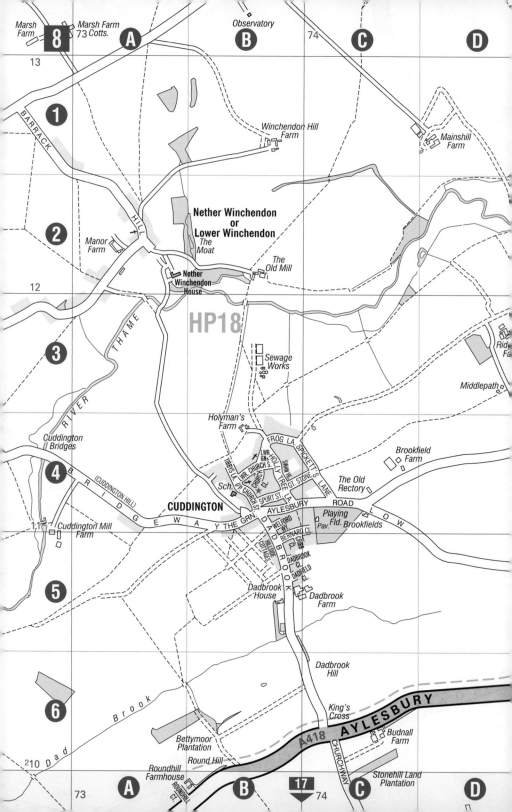

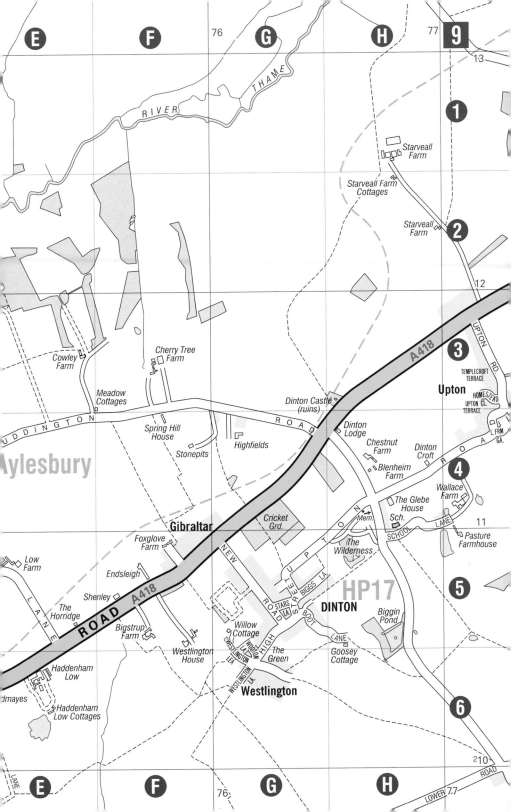

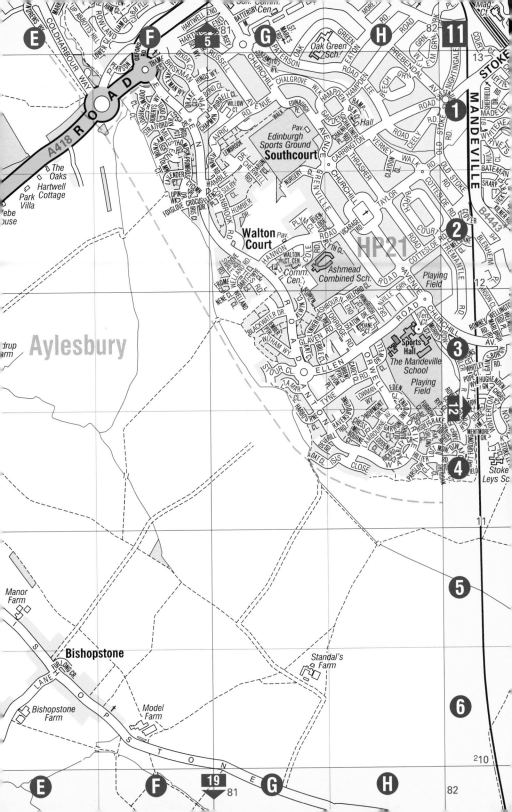

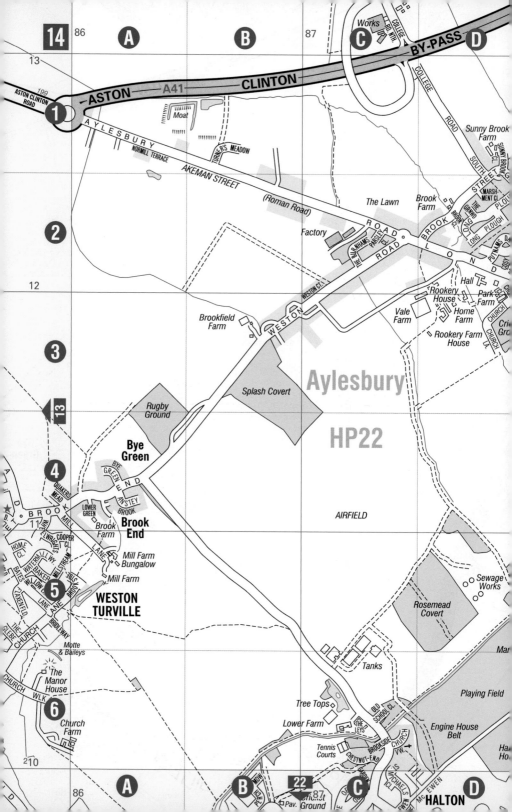

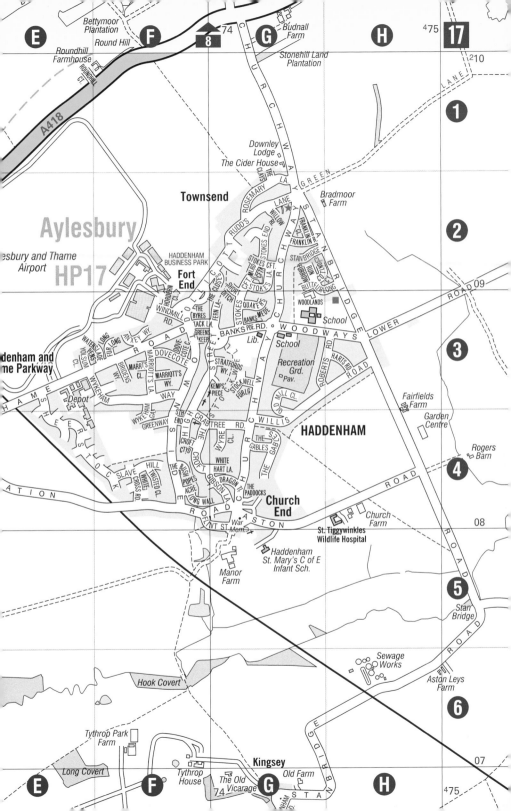

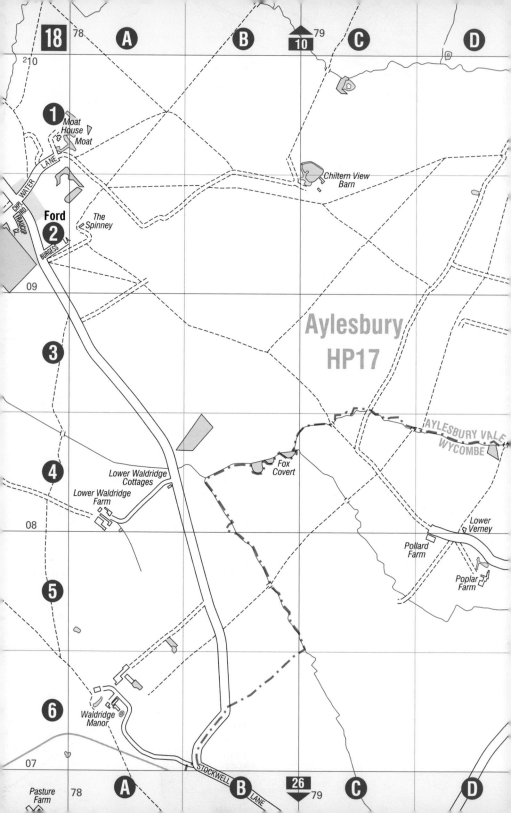

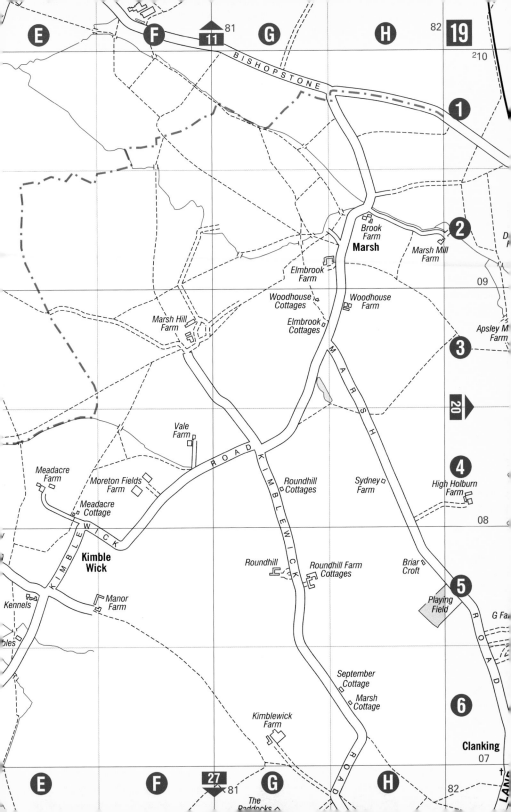

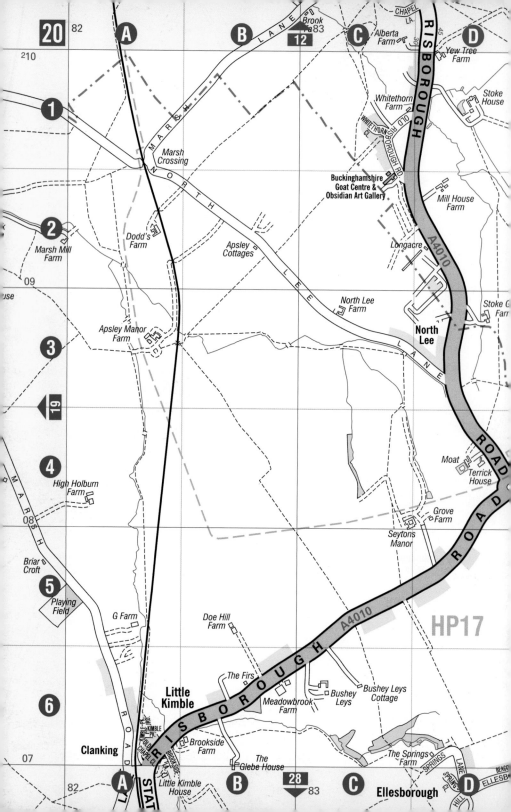

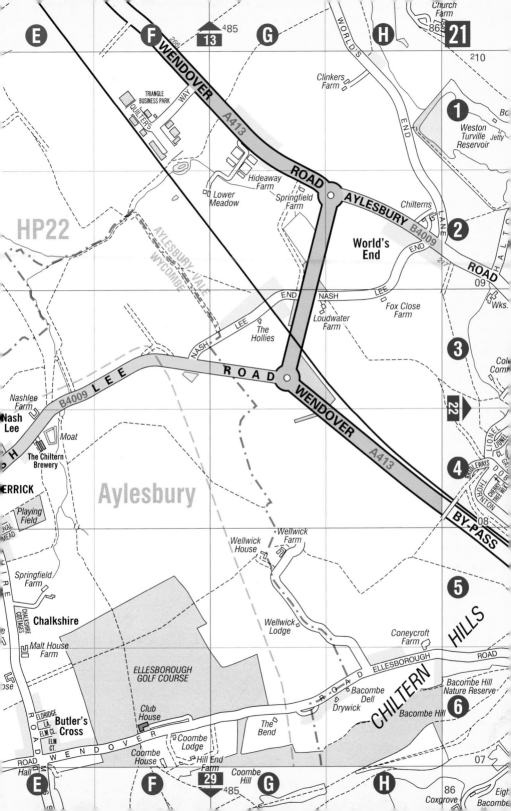

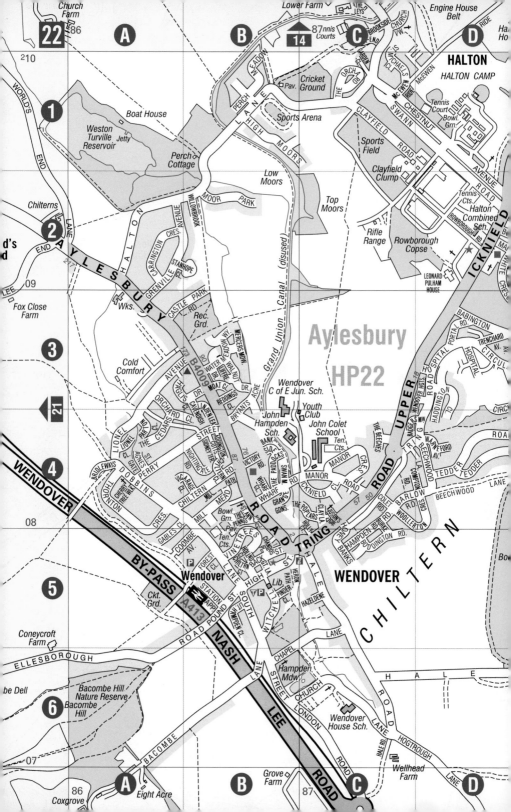

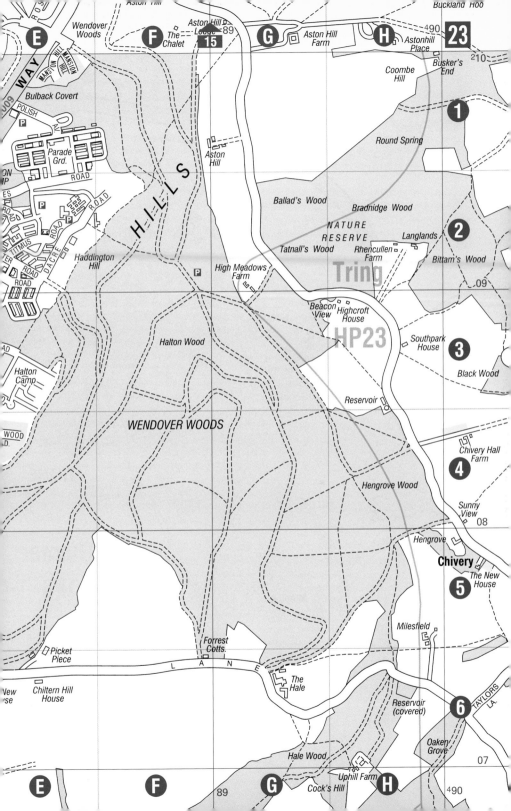

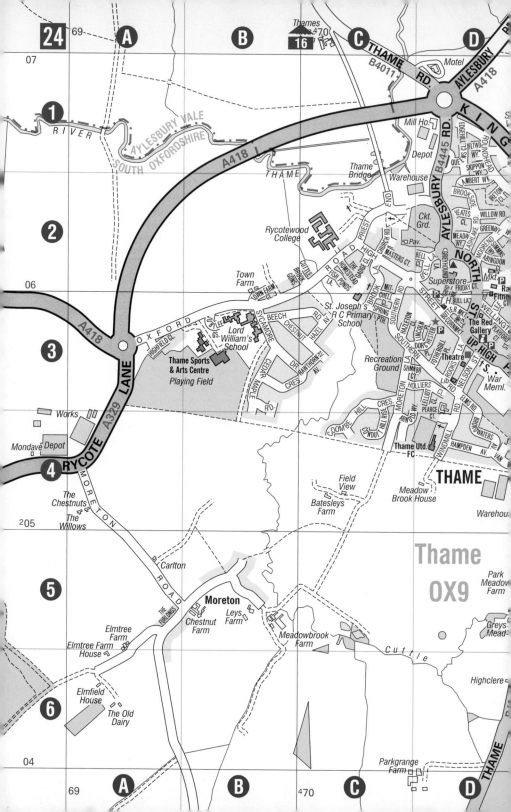

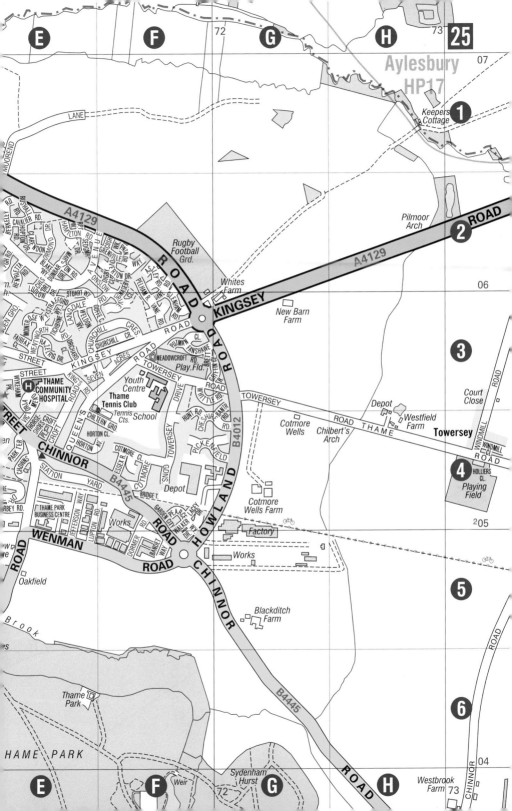

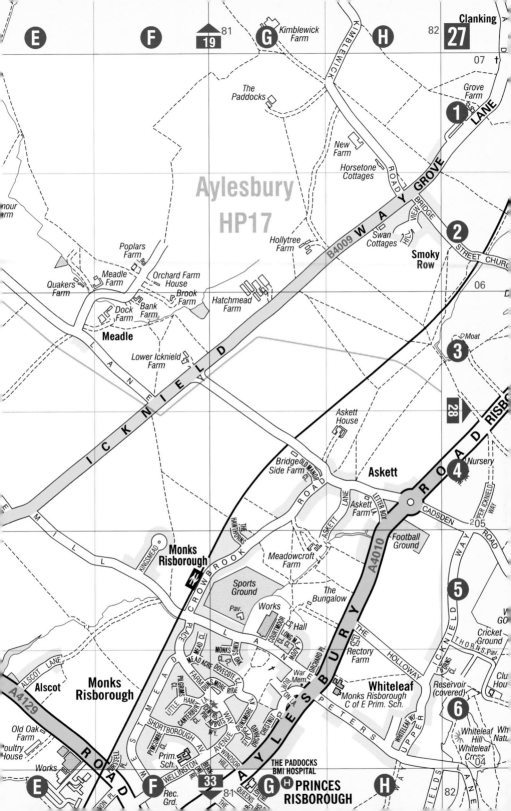

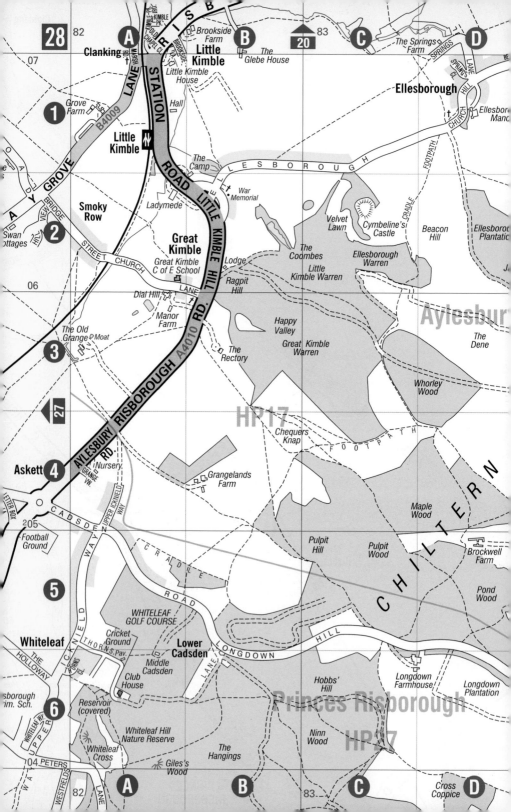

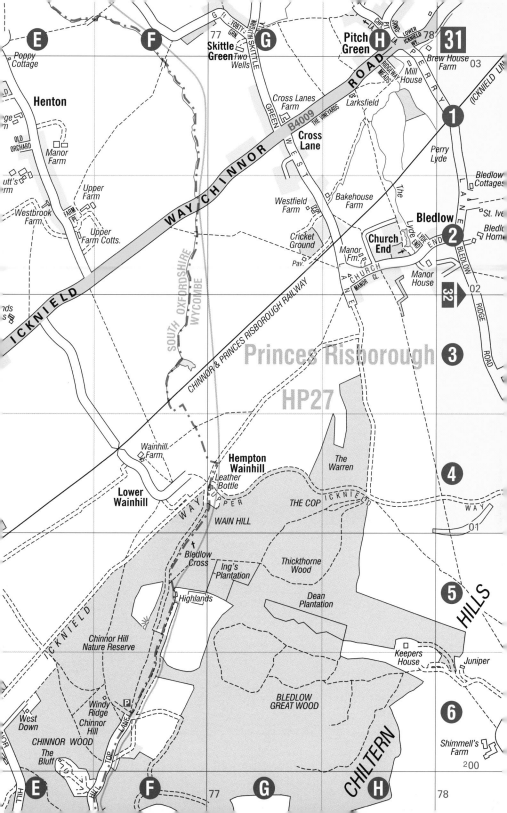

Poppy
Cottage

Henton

OLD
ORCHARD

Manor
Farm

utt's
rm

Westbrook
Farm

Upper
Farm

FARM
PL

Upper
Farm Cotts.

77
Skittle
Green

Two
Wells

FORTY
GRN

NORTH SKITTLE

GREEN WEST

Cross Lanes
Farm

B4009

THE VINEYARDS

CHINNOR

ICKNIELD WAY

WAY CHINNOR ROAD

Pitch
Green

78

Brew House
Farm

03

Mill
House

Larksfield

RIDGEWAY
MEADS

Cross
Lane

Westfield
Farm

Bakehouse
Farm

The

Cricket
Ground

Pav.

Manor
Fm.

Church
End

CHURCH LANE

MANOR CL

LYDE END

Bledlow

Perry
Lyde

St. Ive

Bledlow
Cottages

Bledlo
Hom

Manor
House

1

2

32

02

(ICKNIELD LIN

PERRY LANE

BLEDLOW RIDGE ROAD

SOUTH OXFORDSHIRE

WYCOMBE

ICKNIELD

CHINNOR & PRINCES RISBOROUGH RAILWAY

Princes Risborough

HP27

3

Wainhill
Farm

Hempton
Wainhill

Leather
Bottle

Lower
Wainhill

WAY

UPPER

WAIN HILL

THE COP

ICKNIELD

The
Warren

WAY

01

4

Bledlow
Cross

Ing's
Plantation

Highlands

Thickthorne
Wood

Dean
Plantation

HILLS

5

ICKNIELD

Chinnor Hill
Nature Reserve

Keepers
House

Juniper

West
Down

Windy
Ridge
Chinnor
Hill

CHINNOR WOOD

The
Bluff

TOP LANE

BLEDLOW
GREAT WOOD

Shimmell's
Farm

200

6

CHILTERN

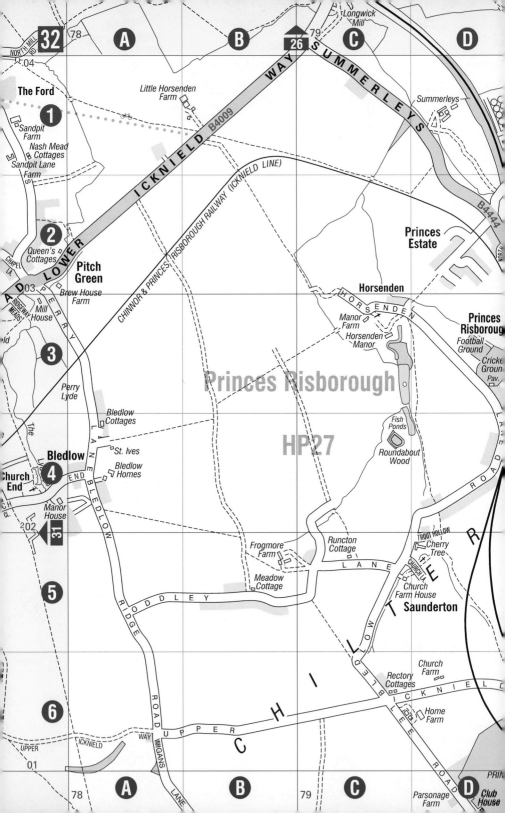

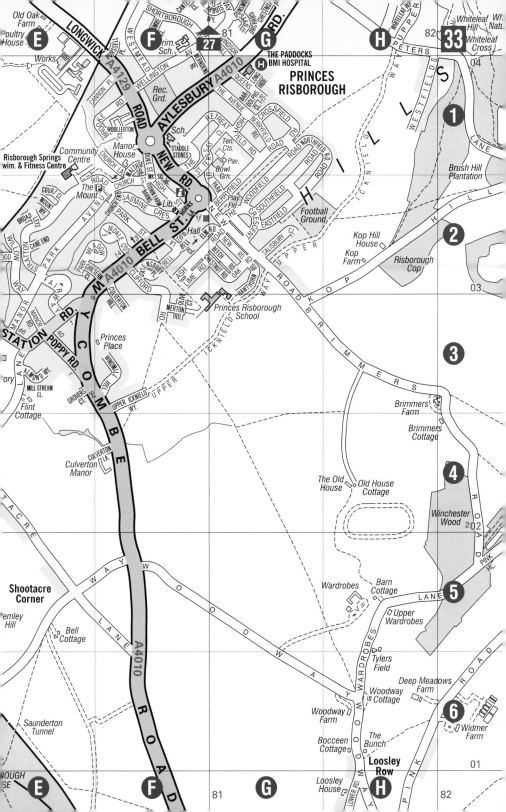

INDEX

Including Streets, Places & Areas, Hospitals & Hospices, Industrial Estates,
Selected Flats & Walkways, Stations, and Selected Places of Interest.

HOW TO USE THIS INDEX

1. Each street name is followed by its Postcode District and then by its Locality abbreviation(s) and then by its map reference;
   e.g. **Abbey Rd.** HP19: Ayle . . . .3F **5** is in the HP19 Postcode District and the Aylesbury Locality and is to be found in square 3F on page **5**.
   The page number is shown in bold type.

2. A strict alphabetical order is followed in which Av., Rd., St., etc. (though abbreviated) are read in full and as part of the street name;
   e.g. **Ash Cl.** appears after **Ashbourne End** but before **Ashford Cl.**

3. Streets and a selection of flats and walkways too small to be shown on the maps, appear in the index with the thoroughfare to which it is connected shown in brackets;
   e.g. **Archways** HP20: Ayle . . . .5H **5** (off Castle St.)

4. Addresses that are in more than one part are referred to as not continuous.

5. Places and areas are shown in the index in BLUE TYPE and the map reference is to the actual map square in which the town centre or area is located and not to the place name shown on the map; e.g. AYLESBURY 5A 6

6. An example of a selected place of interest is Buckinghamshire County Mus., The. 5H 5

7. An example of a station is Aylesbury Station (Rail) 6H 5

8. An example of a hospital is FLORENCE NIGHTINGALE HOUSE (HOSPICE). . . .3B 12

GENERAL ABBREVIATIONS

App. : Approach	**Est.** : Estate	**Lwr.** : Lower	**Sq.** : Square
Av. : Avenue	**Fld.** : Field	**Mnr.** : Manor	**St.** : Street
Bldgs. : Buildings	**Gdns.** : Gardens	**Mkt.** : Market	**Ter.** : Terrace
Bus. : Business	**Ga.** : Gate	**Mdw.** : Meadow	**Trad.** : Trading
Cen. : Centre	**Gt.** : Great	**M.** : Mews	**Up.** : Upper
Cl. : Close	**Grn.** : Green	**Nth.** : North	**Va.** : Vale
Cnr. : Corner	**Gro.** : Grove	**Pde.** : Parade	**Vw.** : View
Cott. : Cottage	**Hgts.** : Heights	**Pk.** : Park	**Vs.** : Villas
Cotts. : Cottages	**Ho.** : House	**Pas.** : Passage	**Wlk.** : Walk
Ct. : Court	**Ind.** : Industrial	**Pl.** : Place	**Yd.** : Yard
Cres. : Crescent	**Info.** : Information	**Ri.** : Rise	
Cft. : Croft	**La.** : Lane	**Rd.** : Road	
Dr. : Drive	**Lit.** : Little	**Sth.** : South	

LOCALITY ABBREVIATIONS

Ask : **Askett**	Dint : **Dinton**	Lit K : **Little Kimble**	Sto : **Stone**
Ast C : **Aston Clinton**	Dray B : **Drayton Beauchamp**	Long C : **Long Crendon**	Syde : **Sydenham**
Ayle : **Aylesbury**	Elle : **Ellesborough**	Long : **Longwick**	Terr : **Terrick**
Bier : **Bierton**	Fleet M : **Fleet Marston**	Loos : **Loosely Row**	Tha : **Thame**
Bish : **Bishopstone**	Ford : **Ford**	Mars : **Marsh**	Tow : **Towersey**
Bled : **Bledlow**	Gt Kim : **Great Kimble**	Mead : **Meadle**	Tring : **Tring**
Bled R : **Bledlow Ridge**	Hadd : **Haddenham**	Mon R : **Monks Risborough**	Upt : **Upton**
Bro : **Broughton**	Halt : **Halton**	More : **Moreton**	Wend : **Wendover**
Buck : **Buckland**	Hart : **Hartwell**	Net W : **Nether Winchendon**	West T : **Weston Turville**
But X : **Butlers Cross**	Hent : **Henton**	Owls : **Owlswick**	Whit : **Whitchurch**
Che : **Chearsley**	Kim W : **Kimble Wick**	Par H : **Parslows Hillock**	Wils : **Wilstone**
Chin : **Chinnor**	King : **Kingsey**	Prin R : **Princes Risborough**	
Crow : **Crowell**	King B : **Kingston Blount**	Saun : **Saunderton**	
Cudd : **Cuddington**	L Grn : **Lacey Green**	Sto M : **Stoke Mandeville**	

A

Abbey Rd. HP19: Ayle 3F 5
Abbot Ridge HP18: Long C 4B 16
Abbots Way HP27: Mon R 6G 27
Abbotts Cl. HP20: Ayle 4A 6
Abbotts Rd. HP20: Ayle 4A 6
Abbot Wlk. HP18: Long C 4B 16
Abingdon Cl. OX9: Tha 2D 24
Addington Cotts. HP22: Wend 3B 6
Adkins Cl. HP19: Ayle 2D 4
Aidan Cl. HP21: Ayle 3C 12
Ailward Rd. HP19: Ayle 3D 4
Aiston Pl. HP20: Ayle 3B 6
Albany Pl. HP19: Ayle 3E 5
Albert St. HP20: Ayle 5C 6
Alderson Cl. HP19: Ayle 3E 5
Alexander Rd. HP20: Ayle 4H 5
Alham Rd. HP21: Ayle 1G 11
Allonby Way HP19: Ayle 6D 6
Almond Way HP27: Prin R 3E 33
ALSCOT 6E 27
Alscot La. HP27: Prin R 6E 27
Alton Ho. Office Pk. HP19: Ayle . . .4F 5
Alwin Cl. HP21: Ayle 3G 11
Ambleside HP21: Ayle 2D 12
Anchor La. HP20: Ayle 5A 6
Andrews Way HP19: Ayle 6E 5
Angood Cl. HP27: Prin R 2E 33
Angus Rd. HP21: Ayle 2E 5
Anns Cl. HP21: Ayle 3C 12
Anson Cl. HP21: Ayle 3A 12
Anstey Brook HP22: West T 4A 14
Anton Way HP21: Ayle 3G 11
Anxey Way HP17: Hadd 3F 17
Aplin Rd. HP21: Ayle 1E 13
Apsley Ct. HP19: Ayle 4H 5
Aquavale Swimming Cen. 5B 6

Archer Dr. HP20: Ayle 3C 6
Archive Cl. HP22: Ast C 2D 14
Archways HP20: Ayle 5H 5
   (off Castle St.)
Ardenham La. HP19: Ayle 4H 5
Ardenham St. HP19: Ayle 4G 5
Argyle Av. HP19: Ayle 3E 5
Arncott Way HP19: Ayle 4D 4
Arnold Cl. HP22: Sto M 4E 13
Arnold Ct. HP21: Ayle 1B 12
Arnold Way OX9: Tha 4C 24
Arundel Grn. HP20: Ayle 3B 6
Ascott Ct. HP20: Ayle 4A 6
Ascott Rd. HP20: Ayle 4A 6
Ashbourne End HP21: Ayle 3G 11
Ash Cl. HP20: Ayle 3C 6
Ashford Cl. HP21: Ayle 2C 12
Ash Gro. HP21: Ayle 6C 6
Ashley Row HP20: Ayle 4C 6
Ashridge OX39: Chin 5B 30
Ash Rd. HP27: Prin R 2F 33
ASKETT 4H 27
Askett La. HP21: Ask 4H 27
Aspen Cl. HP20: Ayle 3C 6
Astley Rd. OX9: Tha 2F 25
ASTON CLINTON 2D 14
Aston Clinton By-Pass
   HP22: Ast C, Buck 1A 14
Aston Clinton Rd. HP22: West T . . .6F 7
Aston Cl. HP19: Ayle 2E 5
Aston Rd. HP17: Hadd 4G 17
Astronomey Way HP19: Ayle 5E 5
   (off Queensgate)
Austen Pl. HP19: Ayle 3D 4
Autumn Cl. HP19: Ayle 2E 5
Avenue, The HP27: Prin R 1G 33
   OX39: Chin 5D 30
Avocet Way HP19: Ayle 2A 6

Avon Pl. HP21: Ayle 3H 11
AYLESBURY 5A 6
Aylesbury Bus. Cen. HP19: Ayle . . .4F 5
Aylesbury College Sports Cen. . . .6G 5
Aylesbury Ind. Est. HP19: Ayle . . .4G 5
Aylesbury Rd. HP17: Dint, Hadd . . .6C 8
   HP18: Che 1C 16
   HP18: Cudd 4B 8
   HP22: Ast C 1A 14
   HP22: Bier 3C 6
   HP22: Wend 2H 21
   HP27: Ask, Mon R, Prin R 1F 33
   OX9: Hadd, Tha 2D 24
Aylesbury Station (Rail) 6H 5
Aylesbury United FC 2H 5
Ayleswater HP19: Ayle 1A 6
Ayres Cl. HP21: Ayle 1F 11
Ayrshire Cl. HP19: Ayle 2E 5

B

Babington Rd. HP22: Halt 3D 22
Back St. HP22: Wend 5B 22
Bacombe La. HP22: Wend 6A 22
Badgers Mdw. HP22: Halt 4C 22
Badgers Ri. HP17: Sto 2A 10
Badrick Rd. HP19: Ayle 3D 4
Bakers Wlk. HP22: West T 5H 13
Balfour Way HP20: Ayle 3A 6
Ballard Cl. HP21: Ayle 2D 12
Bandet Way OX9: Tha 5F 25
Bankside HP22: Wend 4B 22
Banks Pde. HP17: Hadd 3G 17
Banks Rd. HP17: Hadd 3G 17
Bannister Rd. OX9: Tha 3G 25
Bardolphs Cl. HP27: Prin R 1G 33
Bardon Grn. HP20: Ayle 3A 6
Bar La. HP27: Long, Owls 4B 26

Barley Cl. HP22: West T 5H 13
Barley Cres. HP21: Ayle 4H 11
Barlow Rd. HP22: Wend 4C 22
Barnard Cres. HP21: Ayle 2B 12
Barnett Way HP22: Bier 1D 6
Barn Rd. HP27: Long 5B 26
Barnsbury Av. HP20: Ayle 5D 6
Barrie Cl. HP19: Ayle 3D 4
Base Cl. HP20: Ayle 3C 6
Batchelor Cl. HP20: Ayle 3B 6
Bateman Dr. HP21: Ayle 1A 12
Bates Cl. HP20: Ayle 3B 6
Bates La. HP22: West T 5H 13
Battersby M. HP21: Ayle 6G 5
Batt Furlong HP21: Ayle 4A 12
Beacon Cl. HP17: Sto 2A 10
Beaconsfield Rd.
   HP21: Ayle 6A 6
   HP22: Ast C 2E 15
Beacon Vw. HP17: Elle 1D 28
Bearbrook Cl. HP19: Ayle 6G 5
Beaufort Cl. HP21: Ayle 6F 7
BEDGROVE 2D 12
Bedgrove HP21: Ayle 1E 13
Bedwyn Wlk. HP21: Ayle 3G 11
Beech Cl. HP20: Ayle 2D 6
Beeches, The HP22: Wend 4C 22
Beech Grn. HP21: Ayle 1H 11
Beech Rd. HP27: Prin R 2G 33
   OX9: Tha 3B 24
   OX39: Chin 5C 30
Beechwood Ho. HP22: Ast C 2F 15
   (off Beechwood Way)
Beechwood La.
   HP22: Wend, Halt 4D 22
Beechwood Way HP22: Ast C 2F 15
Belgrave Rd. HP19: Ayle 2D 4
Bell Bus. Pk. HP19: Ayle 4D 4

C

Crosland Rd.—Harvey Rd.

Crosland Rd. HP21: Ayle 1D **12**
Crossfield Rd. HP27: Prin R 1G **33**
CROSS LANE 1G **31**
Crowbrook Rd.
HP27: Mon R 5F **27**
Crowell M. HP19: Ayle 5D **4**
Crowell Rd. OX39: Chin 6B **30**
Crown Leys HP20: Ayle 4H **5**
(not continuous)
Cubb Fld. HP19: Ayle 6F **5**
Cuckoo Way HP19: Ayle 5D **4**
CUDDINGTON 4B **8**
Cuddington Hill
HP18: Cudd 4A **8**
Cuddington Rd. HP18: Dint 4E **9**
Culverton Hill HP27: Prin R 2F **33**
Culverton La. HP27: Prin R 4E **33**
Cumberland Cl. HP21: Ayle 6D **6**
Curlew HP19: Ayle 2B **6**
Cursley Path HP19: Ayle 5E **5**
Cuttle Brook Gdns.
OX9: Tha 2B **24**
Cyclamen Pl. HP21: Ayle 2F **11**

D

Dacre Rd. HP22: Halt 2E **23**
Dadbrook HP18: Cudd 4B **8**
Dadbrook Cl. HP18: Cudd 5B **8**
Dadfield Cl. HP18: Cudd 5B **8**
Dalesford Rd. HP21: Ayle 3C **12**
Dalston Cl. HP20: Ayle 3B **6**
Dalwood M. HP19: Ayle 5E **5**
Daly Way HP20: Ayle 6D **6**
Dancers End La.
HP23: Tring 4H **15**
Dane Ct. HP21: Ayle 3H **11**
Dark La. HP18: Che 1C **16**
Darley Cl. HP21: Ayle 1D **12**
Dart Cl. HP21: Ayle 2G **11**
David Cl. HP21: Ayle 3C **12**
Davies Cl. HP20: Ayle 5H **5**
Dawney Cl. HP19: Ayle 3G **5**
Dean Cl. HP21: Ayle 2C **12**
Dean Way HP22: Ast C 3F **15**
Dearing Cl. HP20: Ayle 3B **6**
Delamere Cl. HP20: Ayle 3B **6**
Dell, The HP20: Ayle 3C **6**
Denbigh Rd. OX9: Tha 2E **25**
Denby Wlk. HP20: Ayle 5C **6**
Dennis Cl. HP22: Ast C 3G **15**
Derwent Rd. HP21: Ayle 1D **12**
Desborough Grn.
*HP20: Ayle 3H **5***
(off Dusham La.)
Devereux Pl. HP19: Ayle 3E **5**
Deverill Rd. HP21: Ayle 4G **11**
Devon Rd. HP19: Ayle 2E **5**
Diane Cl. HP21: Ayle 3C **12**
Diane Wlk. HP21: Ayle 3C **12**
Dickens Way HP19: Ayle 3D **4**
Dicks Way HP19: Ayle 2D **4**
Digby Cl. OX9: Tha 2F **25**
DINTON 5G **9**
Dinton Castle (ruins) 3H **9**
Disraeli Sq. HP19: Ayle 5E **5**
Ditchingham Cl. HP19: Ayle 6F **5**
Dixon Cl. HP21: Ayle 1F **11**
Dobbins La. HP22: Wend 4A **22**
Dollicott HP17: Hadd 3F **17**
Dolphin Pl. HP21: Ayle 1A **12**
Dorchester Cl. HP22: Sto M 5D **12**
Dorchester Pl. OX9: Tha 3D **24**
Dormer Cl. HP21: Ayle 1F **11**
Dormer Ct. HP20: Ayle 3B **6**
Dormer Rd. OX9: Tha 5F **25**
Dorrels Rd. HP27: Long 5B **26**
Dorset Pl. HP21: Ayle 1E **13**
Douglas Rd. HP20: Ayle 3B **6**
Dove Cl. HP21: Ayle 2G **11**
Dovecote HP17: Hadd 3F **17**
Dovecote Cl. HP17: Hadd 3F **17**
HP27: Mon R 6G **27**
Dove Ho. *HP19: Ayle 1B **6***
(off Dove Pl.)
Doveleat OX39: Chin 4D **30**
Dove Pl. HP19: Ayle 1B **6**
Dover Hedge HP21: Ayle 6E **7**
Dragon Tail HP17: Hadd 4G **17**
Drake Cl. HP21: Ayle 1F **11**
Drakes Dr. HP18: Long C 5B **16**
Drakes Farm HP18: Long C 4C **16**
DRAYTON BEAUCHAMP 2H **15**
Drayton Rd. HP20: Ayle 3H **5**
Druids Wlk. OX39: Chin 5C **30**
Dryden Cl. HP20: Ayle 3A **6**
Duck Farm Ct. HP20: Ayle 5H **5**
Duck Sq. OX39: Chin 4C **30**
Duke St. HP27: Prin R 1F **33**
Dunbar Dr. OX9: Tha 2E **25**
Dunsham La. HP19: Ayle 2B **6**
HP20: Ayle 3H **5**
DUNSMORE 4H **29**
Dunsmore Av. HP27: Mon R 6G **27**
Dunsmore Ride HP27: Mon R 6F **27**

E

Eagles Rd. HP20: Ayle 5C **6**
Eames Cl. HP20: Ayle 2B **6**
Earlswood Cl. HP21: Ayle 2C **12**
Eastcote Rd. HP21: Ayle 3D **12**
Eastern St. HP20: Ayle 4A **6**
Eastfield Rd. HP20: Ayle 5D **6**
HP27: Prin R 2G **33**
East St. OX9: Tha 3E **25**
Eaton Rd. HP21: Ayle 1H **11**
Ebble Cl. HP21: Ayle 3G **11**
Eden Cl. HP21: Ayle 3H **11**
Edgecombe Rd. HP21: Ayle 2D **12**
Edgehill OX9: Tha 1D **24**
Edinburgh Pl. HP21: Ayle 1G **11**
Edison Rd. HP19: Ayle 4C **4**
Edward Cl. HP21: Ayle 3C **12**
Edward Wlk. HP21: Ayle 3C **12**
Eeles Cl. HP19: Ayle 2D **4**
Egypt Way HP19: Ayle 5E **5**
Elderdene OX39: Chin 3D **30**
Eldridge La. HP17: But X 6E **21**
Eleanor Gdns. HP21: Ayle 2B **12**
Elham Way HP21: Ayle 3C **12**
Eliot Cl. HP19: Ayle 3D **4**
Elizabeth Cl. HP21: Ayle 3D **12**
Ellen Pl. HP21: Ayle 2G **11**
Ellen Rd. HP21: Ayle 1F **11**
Ellen Wlk. *HP21: Ayle 1F **11***
(off Ellen Rd.)
ELLESBOROUGH 1D **28**
Ellesborough Rd.
HP17: But X, Elle, Lit K 2B **28**
HP22: Wend 6H **21**
Elm Brook Cl. HP18: Che 2D **16**
Elm Cl. HP17: But X 6E **21**
HP22: West T 5H **13**
OX39: Chin 6C **30**
Elm Ct. HP17: But X 6E **21**
Elmdale Gdns. HP27: Prin R 2F **33**
Elm Dr. OX39: Chin 6C **30**
Elm Farm Rd. HP21: Ayle 2B **12**
Elm Grn. HP21: Ayle 1H **11**
ELMHURST 2A **6**
Elmhurst Rd. HP20: Ayle 3H **5**
Elm Rd. HP27: Prin R 2F **33**
Elms, The HP20: Ayle 3A **6**
Elms Rd. OX9: Tha 3D **24**
Elm Trees HP18: Long C 2A **16**
Elsmore Cl. HP21: Ayle 3D **12**
Ember Path HP21: Ayle 3G **11**
EMMINGTON 1A **30**
Emmington OX39: Chin 2A **30**
Enborne Cl. HP21: Ayle 3H **11**
Ensbury Path HP20: Ayle 3A **6**
Eskdale Rd. HP22: Sto M 5D **12**
Essex Ho. HP20: Ayle 4H **5**
Essex Pl. HP19: Ayle 2E **5**
Essex Rd. OX9: Tha 4F **25**
Estover Way OX39: Chin 5B **30**
Evans Cl. HP18: Che 1C **16**
HP21: Ayle 3C **12**
Evenlode Cl. HP21: Ayle 2G **11**
Evesham Grn. HP19: Ayle 2G **5**
Evett Cl. HP20: Ayle 4B **6**
Exchange St. HP20: Ayle 5A **6**
Eyre Cl. HP19: Ayle 5D **4**
Eythrope Rd. HP17: Sto 1A **10**

F

Fairfax Cl. OX9: Tha 3E **25**
Fairfax Cres. HP20: Ayle 3A **6**
FAIRFORD LEYS 5D **4**
Fairford Leys Way HP19: Ayle 6E **5**
Fair Mile HP21: Ayle 6B **6**
Fairway HP27: Prin R 2E **33**
Faithfull Cl. HP17: Sto 2A **10**
Falcon, The HP19: Ayle 1B **6**
Fall Cl. HP19: Ayle 2H **5**
Fanshawe Rd. OX9: Tha 3F **25**
Faraday Rd. HP19: Ayle 4E **5**
Far Furlong Cl. HP21: Ayle 4H **11**
Farmbrough Cl. HP20: Ayle 4C **6**
Farm Pl. OX39: Hent 2E **31**
Farnley Rd. HP20: Ayle 3A **6**
Fells Cl. HP18: Long C 3B **16**
Fern La. HP17: Hadd 3G **17**
Field Cl. HP20: Ayle 3C **6**
Field End HP18: Long C 4C **16**
Fieldfare HP19: Ayle 1A **6**
Field Way HP20: Ayle 3C **6**
Finmere Cres. HP21: Ayle 2E **13**
Firecrest Way HP19: Ayle 4D **4**
Firs, The HP22: Bier 1E **7**
Firs Ct. HP22: Bier 1E **7**
Fish Ponds La. OX9: Tha 2C **24**
Flaxen Fld. HP22: West T 5H **13**
FLEET MARSTON 1A **4**
Fleet St. HP20: Ayle 4H **5**
Fleetwood Way OX9: Tha 1D **24**
Fletcher Cl. HP19: Ayle 2D **4**
Flint Hollow OX39: Chin 5B **30**
Flint St. HP17: Hadd 4F **17**
Florence Ct. *HP19: Ayle 4H **5***
(off Willow Rd.)
FLORENCE NIGHTINGALE HOUSE
(HOSPICE) *3B 12*
(within Stoke Mandeville Hospital)
FORD 2A **18**
Ford Rd. HP17: Ford, Sto 6A **10**
Forest Cl. HP22: Wend 5B **22**
*HP27: Prin R 2G **33***
(off Chestnut Rd.)
Foresters OX39: Chin 5B **30**
FORT END 2F **17**
Forty Grn. HP27: Bled 1G **31**
Foster Cl. HP20: Ayle 3B **6**
Fothergill Pl. OX9: Tha 3D **24**
Fountain Ct. *HP20: Ayle 5H **5***
(off Buckingham St.)
Fowler Rd. HP19: Ayle 5F **5**
Fox Cover OX39: Chin 5C **30**
Foxglove HP21: Ayle 2F **11**
Franklin Cl. HP17: Hadd 2G **17**
Franklin Rd. HP17: Hadd 2G **17**
Fraucup Cl. HP17: Ford 2A **18**
Fremantle Rd. HP21: Ayle 2A **12**
Friarage Pas. HP20: Ayle 5H **5**
Friarage Rd. HP20: Ayle 5H **5**
Friarscroft Way HP20: Ayle 5G **5**
Friars Furlong HP18: Long C 2A **16**
Friars Sq. HP20: Ayle 5H **5**
Friday Ct. OX9: Tha 2D **24**
Frog La. HP18: Cudd 4B **8**
Frogmore La. HP18: Long C 4A **16**
Frome Cl. HP21: Ayle 2G **11**
Fulmar Pl. *HP19: Ayle 2B **6***
(off Watermeadow)
Furlong Cres. HP17: Bish 6E **11**
Furlongs, The OX9: More 5A **24**
Furrow Cl. HP21: Ayle 3H **11**

G

Gables, The HP17: Hadd 4G **17**
Gables Cl. HP22: Wend 5A **22**
Gadge Cl. OX9: Tha 2C **24**
Gainsborough Pl. HP19: Ayle 2D **4**
Gainsborough Rd. HP21: Ayle 3A **12**
Gala Bingo
Aylesbury 5A **6**
Galloway HP19: Ayle 2E **5**
Galsworthy Pl. HP19: Ayle 3D **4**
Garden City OX9: Tha 4F **25**
Garden Cl. HP22: Halt 1C **22**
Gardner Cl. HP19: Ayle 2E **5**
Garland Way HP22: Ast C 2E **15**
Garron Cl. HP21: Ayle 4H **11**
Gas Alley OX9: Tha 3E **25**
Gatehouse Cl. HP19: Ayle 5G **5**
Gatehouse Rd. HP19: Ayle 4G **5**
Gatehouse Way HP19: Ayle 4F **5**
Gatensbury Pl. HP27: Prin R 2F **33**
George St. HP20: Ayle 5H **5**
Gib La. HP22: Bier 1F **7**
GIBRALTAR 4F **9**
Gibson La. HP17: Hadd 4G **17**
Giffard Way HP18: Long C 2A **16**
Gilmore Rd. HP20: Ayle 2A **6**
Gingers Cl. HP22: Ast C 2E **15**
Glaven Rd. HP21: Ayle 3G **11**
Glebe, The HP17: Sto 2A **10**
HP22: West T 5H **13**
Glenfield Cl. HP21: Ayle 2C **12**
Glenham Rd. OX9: Tha 3F **25**
Glynswood OX39: Chin 5C **30**
Goffe Cl. OX9: Tha 3F **25**
Gogh Rd. HP19: Ayle 3C **4**
Goldcrest HP19: Ayle 1A **6**
Golden Hills OX39: Chin 5D **30**
Goodsen Ind. M. OX9: Tha 3D **24**
Goodwin Rd. HP19: Ayle 5G **5**
Goosen Grn. HP21: Ayle 1E **13**
Gowers Fld. HP20: Ayle 4H **5**
Goya Pl. HP19: Ayle 3D **4**
Grafton Orchard OX39: Chin 4D **30**
Grafton Rd. HP19: Ayle 3E **5**
Granary Yd. HP18: Long C 3A **16**
Grange Gdns. HP22: Wend 4B **22**
Grange Sports Cen., The 6B **6**
Grange Vw. HP27: Ask 4A **28**
Granville Pl. HP20: Ayle 5H **5**
Granville St. HP20: Ayle 5H **5**
Grasmere HP21: Ayle 2D **12**
Grass Hays HP21: Ayle 6E **7**
Grasslands HP20: Ayle 4C **6**
GREAT KIMBLE 2B **28**
Great La. HP22: Bier 1C **6**
HP22: Wend 5B **22**
Great Mdw. Way HP19: Ayle 5D **4**
Great Stone HP18: Cudd 4B **8**
Gt. Western St. HP20: Ayle 5H **5**
Grebe Cl. HP19: Ayle 2B **6**
Grecian St. HP20: Ayle 5C **6**
Green, The HP18: Che 1C **16**
HP18: Cudd 4B **8**
HP27: Long 5B **26**
Green Acre HP21: Ayle 6C **6**
Green End HP20: Ayle 5H **5**
Green End St. HP22: Ast C 2D **14**
Green La. HP17: Hadd 6E **9**
HP27: Long 2A **26**
Greens Keep HP17: Hadd 3F **17**
Green Vw. HP20: Ayle 3C **6**
Greenway HP17: Hadd 4F **17**
OX9: Tha 2D **24**
Greenwood, The HP22: Ast C 2D **14**
Greenwood Av. OX39: Chin 6C **30**
Greenwood Mdw. OX39: Chin 5D **30**
Greetham Rd. HP21: Ayle 1E **13**
Grendon Way HP22: Bier 1C **6**
Grenville Av. HP22: Wend 3A **22**
Grenville Grn. HP21: Ayle 3H **11**
Grenville Rd. HP21: Ayle 2G **11**
Grenville Way OX9: Tha 2F **25**
Greyhound La. OX9: Tha 2D **24**
Greyhound Wlk. OX9: Tha 2D **24**
Griffin Ind. Mall HP19: Ayle 4F **5**
Griffin La. HP19: Ayle 4F **5**
Griffin Rd. OX9: Tha 3G **25**
Griffiths Acre HP17: Sto 2C **10**
Grimmer Cl. HP19: Ayle 2D **4**
Grove Ct. HP22: Bier 1E **7**
Grove La. HP17: Gt Kim, Lit K 2H **27**
Grovers Ct. HP27: Prin R 3E **33**
Groves Rd. HP22: Halt 2E **23**
Guernsey Cl. HP19: Ayle 2E **5**
Guillemot Ct. HP19: Ayle 2A **6**
Guillemot Way HP19: Ayle 2A **6**
Gull Way HP19: Ayle 2B **6**
Gurney Cl. HP20: Ayle 3B **6**
Guttman Rd. HP21: Ayle 2B **12**

H

HADDENHAM 3F **17**
Haddenham and Thame Parkway Station
(Rail) 3E **17**
Haddenham Bus. Pk.
HP17: Hadd 2F **17**
Haddenham Rd. HP17: King 6G **17**
Haddington Cl. HP22: Halt 4D **22**
Haddington Way HP20: Ayle 4C **6**
Haggar St. HP17: Sto 2A **10**
Haglis Dr. HP22: Wend 3A **22**
Hailey Cft. OX39: Chin 5B **30**
Haines Cl. HP19: Ayle 3D **4**
Hale La. HP22: Wend 6C **22**
Hale Leys Cen. HP20: Ayle 5A **6**
Hale Rd. HP22: Wend 5C **22**
Hales Cres. HP21: Ayle 3D **12**
Hale St. HP20: Ayle 5A **6**
HALTON 1C **22**
Halton La. HP22: Wend, Halt 2A **22**
Halton Wood Rd. HP22: Halt 4E **23**
Hambledon Cl. HP21: Ayle 2D **12**
Hamble Dr. HP21: Ayle 2G **11**
Hamilton Ct. HP19: Ayle 3H **5**
Hamilton Ho. *HP19: Ayle 4E **5***
(off Broadfields)
Hamilton Rd. OX9: Tha 2E **25**
Hampden Av. OX9: Tha 4D **24**
Hampden Cl. HP21: Ayle 1H **11**
HP22: Sto M 6D **12**
Hampden Gdns. HP21: Ayle 1H **11**
Hampden Rd. HP21: Ayle 1H **11**
HP22: Sto M 5D **12**
HP22: Wend 5C **22**
Hampden Sq. HP19: Ayle 5E **5**
Hannon Rd. HP21: Ayle 2G **11**
Hanover Cl. HP19: Ayle 3E **5**
Hanover Ct. *HP21: Ayle 6A **6***
(off Croft Rd.)
Hanson Way HP21: Ayle 3C **12**
Harbourne Cl. HP21: Ayle 4G **11**
Harcourt Grn. HP19: Ayle 3F **5**
Hardy Cl. HP21: Ayle 6A **6**
Harebridge La. HP22: Halt 5E **15**
Harrier Cl. HP19: Ayle 2B **6**
Harris Cl. HP20: Ayle 3B **6**
Harrison Pl. OX9: Tha 2D **24**
Harroell HP18: Long C 3B **16**
(not continuous)
Harrow Cl. HP21: Ayle 3A **12**
Harts Rd. HP17: Hadd 3H **17**
HARTWELL 2D **10**
Hartwell End HP21: Ayle 6F **5**
(not continuous)
Harvey Rd. HP21: Ayle 2A **12**

36 A-Z Aylesbury

Melbourne Cl.—Roberts Way

Melbourne Cl. HP21: Ayle 2A 12
Melford Grn. HP19: Ayle 2G 5
Mellstock Rd. HP21: Ayle 2B 12
Melrose Wlk. HP21: Ayle 2B 12
Mentmore Grn. HP21: Ayle 4A 12
Mercers Mdw. HP22: Wend 3B 22
Meredith Dr. HP19: Ayle 3D 4
Merlin Cen. HP19: Ayle 5G 5
Merton Rd. HP27: Prin R 3F 33
Messenger Cl. HP21: Ayle 1C 12
Michaels M. HP19: Ayle 5E 5
Middle Fld. HP22: West T 4H 13
Middle Rd. HP21: Ayle 6D 6
Middle Way OX39: Chin 5B 30
Midhurst Cl. HP21: Ayle 2D 12
Milennium Point HP19: Ayle 4E 5
Miles Cl. HP21: Ayle 6C 6
Miles Ct. HP22: Bier 2D 6
Miles End HP21: Ayle 1F 11
Millers Turn OX39: Chin 5B 30
Millers Way HP19: Ayle 5E 5
Mill La. HP22: West T 4H 13
HP27: Mon R 5E 27
OX39: Chin 5A 30
Mill Mead HP22: Wend 4B 22
Mill M. HP19: Ayle 5F 5
Mill Path HP22: Wend 4B 22
Millstream HP22: West T 5H 13
Mill Stream Cl. HP27: Prin R 3E 33
Mill St. HP20: Ayle 4A 6
Mill Way HP20: Ayle 5G 5
Milton Gdns. HP27: Prin R 3E 33
Milton Rd. HP21: Ayle 1B 12
HP22: Ast C 2F 15
Mimosa Ct. *HP21: Ayle 1F 11*
(off Primrose Dr.)
Misbourne Cl. HP21: Ayle 4H 11
Missenden Rd. HP17: But X 1E 29
Mitcham Wlk. HP19: Ayle 3E 5
Mitch Cl. HP20: Ayle 6D 6
Mitchell Cl. OX9: Tha 3C 24
Moat Cl. HP22: Wend 3B 22
Moat End HP22: Bier 1D 6
Moat's Cres. OX9: Tha 3E 25
Monet Pl. HP19: Ayle 3C 4
Monks Path *HP19: Ayle 5E 5*
(off Hemp Hill)
MONKS RISBOROUGH 6G 27
Monks Risborough Station (Rail) 5F 27
Monmouth Cl. HP19: Ayle 3E 5
Montague Rd. HP21: Ayle 6H 5
Montesson Sq. *OX9: Tha 3D 24*
(off Up. High St.)
Montrose Way OX9: Tha 3E 25
Moor End La. OX9: Tha 1E 25
(Cromwell Av.)
OX9: Tha 2D 24
(North St.)
Moorhen Ct. HP19: Ayle 2A 6
Moor Pk. HP22: Wend 2B 22
More Av. HP21: Ayle 6H 5
MORETON 5B 24
Moreton La. HP17: Bish 6E 11
OX9: Tha 3C 24
Moreton Rd. OX9: More 4A 24
Morris Ct. HP21: Ayle 3H 11
Mount Cl. HP22: Ast C 3F 15
Mount Pl. HP19: Ayle 4H 5
Mount St. HP20: Ayle 5H 5
Mount Way HP27: Prin R 2E 33
Mowbray Rd. HP20: Ayle 3H 5
Mullins Way HP19: Ayle 3C 4
Musgrave Rd. OX39: Chin 4D 30

N

Nappin Cl. HP19: Ayle 2D 4
Nappins Cl. HP18: Long C 3B 16
Narbeth Dr. HP20: Ayle 5D 6
Naseby Cl. OX9: Tha 2F 25
Nash Cl. HP21: Ayle 3C 12
NASH LEE 4E 21
Nash Lee End HP22: Wend 3F 21
Nash Lee Rd. HP17: Terr 4E 21
HP22: Wend 5B 22
Needlemakers HP18: Long C 2B 16
Nelson St. OX9: Tha 3D 24
Nelson Ter. HP20: Ayle 5H 5
Nene Cl. HP21: Ayle 3G 11
Nether Winchendon House 2A 8
NETHER WINCHENDON 2A 8
New Cl. Farm Rd. OX39: Hent 1C 30
Newell Cl. HP21: Ayle 1C 12
New Mdw. HP21: Ayle 1E 13
New Rd. HP17: Dint 5G 9
HP22: Ast C 2E 15
HP22: West T 1F 13
HP27: Prin R 1F 33
(not continuous)
New St. HP20: Ayle 4H 5
Neyland Dr. HP19: Ayle 2G 5
Nightingale Rd. HP21: Ayle 1A 12
HP22: Wend 4B 22
Norfolk Ter. HP20: Ayle 4A 6
Normill Ter. HP22: Ast C 1A 14
North Dr. HP21: Ayle 2A 12
Nth. Eastern Rd. HP19: Ayle 3G 5
Northern Rd. HP19: Ayle 4G 5
Northfield Rd. HP20: Ayle 5D 6
HP27: Prin R 1G 33
NORTH LEE 3D 20
Nth. Lee La. HP22: Terr 2A 20
Northmill HP27: Prin R 2D 32
Nth. Mill Rd. HP27: Bled 6A 26
North St. OX9: Tha 2D 24
Northumberland Av. HP21: Ayle 1D 12
Norwood Cl. HP20: Ayle 3B 6
Nursery Cl. HP21: Ayle 2G 11
Nuthatch HP19: Ayle 2B 6

O

Oak End Way OX39: Chin 6D 30
Oak Farm Rare Breeds Pk. 5F 7
Oakfield Rd. HP20: Ayle 5C 6
Oak Grn. HP21: Ayle 6G 5
OAKLEY 6C 30
Oakley La. OX39: Chin 5B 30
Oakley Rd. OX39: Chin 6B 30
Oak Rd. HP27: Prin R 2G 33
Oat Cl. HP21: Ayle 4G 11
Oddley La. HP27: Saun 5A 32
Odeon Cinema Aylesbury 5A 6
O'Grady Way HP19: Ayle 2E 5
Old Brewery Cl. HP21: Ayle 6A 6
Old Burrs HP21: Ayle 4H 11
Old Chapel Cl. HP17: Lit K 6A 20
Old Forge Gdns. HP22: Bier 1D 6
Oldhams Mdw. HP20: Ayle 3B 6
Oldmanor Cl. HP27: Ask 4G 27
Old Mill Cl. HP17: Hadd 3G 17
Old Orchard OX39: Hent 1E 31
Old Orchards HP22: Bier 2C 6
Old Plough Cl. HP18: Che 1C 16
Old Risborough Rd. HP22: Sto M 1C 20
Old School Cl. HP22: Halt 6C 14
Old Stoke Rd. HP21: Ayle 2A 12
Old Windmill Way HP18: Long C 2A 16
Oliffe Cl. HP20: Ayle 2H 5
Oliffe Way HP20: Ayle 2H 5
Olivier Way HP20: Ayle 5C 6
Onslow Dr. OX9: Tha 2F 25
Orchard, The HP22: Ast C 2E 15
HP22: Halt 1C 22
Orchard Cl. HP20: Ayle 2B 6
HP22: Sto M 5D 12
(not continuous)
HP22: Wend 3A 22
HP27: Long 4B 26
OX9: Tha 3E 25
Orchard Dr. HP22: Ast C 2E 15
Orchard Pl. HP27: Mon R 6G 27
Orchards, The HP17: Sto 2A 10
Orchard Way HP20: Ayle 3B 6
OX39: Chin 5C 30
Ormesby Cl. HP21: Ayle 2C 12
Ormond Dr. OX9: Tha 2E 25
Orwell Cl. HP21: Ayle 3H 11
Orwell Dr. HP21: Ayle 3H 11
Osier Way HP20: Ayle 5B 6
Osprey, The HP19: Ayle 1A 6
Osprey Wlk. HP19: Ayle 1A 6
Otway Cl. HP21: Ayle 4A 12
Oulton Cl. HP21: Ayle 2C 12
Overstrand HP22: Ast C 2E 15
Overton Dr. OX9: Tha 2F 25
Owl Cl. HP19: Ayle 2B 6
OWLSWICK 2B 26
Owlswick La. HP27: Owls 3C 26
Oxford Rd. HP17: Hart, Sto 2A 10
HP19: Ayle 6F 5
HP21: Ayle 6F 5
OX9: Tha 3A 24

P

Paddock, The HP21: Ayle 6E 7
PADDOCKS BMI HOSPITAL, THE 1G 33
Paddocks, The HP17: Hadd 4G 17
HP22: Wend 4B 22
Padstow Cl. HP20: Ayle 4B 6
Pakenham Cl. HP19: Ayle 5D 4
Palmer Av. HP19: Ayle 4G 5
Park Ct. OX9: Tha 3E 25
Parker Wlk. HP19: Ayle 2H 5
Park Mdw. HP27: Prin R 2E 33
Park St. HP20: Ayle 4A 6
HP27: Prin R 2F 33
OX9: Tha 3D 24
Park St. Ind. Est. HP20: Ayle 4B 6
Park Ter. OX9: Tha 4E 25
Park Vw. HP22: Ast C 3E 15
Parliament Rd. OX9: Tha 2D 24
Parmiter Cl. HP19: Ayle 5F 5
Parrot Cl. HP21: Ayle 1F 11
Parsley Cl. HP22: Ast C 2C 14
Parslow Cl. HP21: Ayle 4H 11
Parslow Ct. *HP21: Ayle 4H 11*
(off Sheridan Cl.)
Parson's Fee HP20: Ayle 5H 5
Parsons La. HP22: Bier 2D 6
Parton Cl. HP22: Wend 4A 22
Parton Rd. HP20: Ayle 5D 6
Partridge Way HP19: Ayle 2B 6
Pastures, The HP20: Ayle 3D 6
Paterson Rd. HP21: Ayle 6G 5
Patrick Way HP21: Ayle 2C 12
Pavers Ct. HP21: Ayle 4H 11
Pavilion Cl. HP20: Ayle 5C 6
Pearce Cl. HP21: Ayle 3A 12
Pearce Ct. OX9: Tha 3D 24
Pearce Way OX9: Tha 4F 25
Pearson Cl. HP19: Ayle 1F 11
Peascroft HP18: Long C 3B 16
Pecks Farm Cl. HP22: Bier 1E 7
Peeble La. HP20: Ayle 5H 5
Peggs La. HP22: Buck 2F 15
Pelham Rd. OX9: Tha 2F 25
Pemberton Cl. HP21: Ayle 2B 12
Pembroke Rd. HP20: Ayle 4B 6
Penfold HP22: West T 5H 13
Penley Cl. OX39: Chin 5B 30
Pennefather Ct. HP21: Ayle 6A 6
Pennings, The HP22: Wend 4B 22
Pennington Dr. OX9: Tha 2F 25
Penn Rd. HP21: Ayle 6H 5
Penrith Way HP21: Ayle 6D 6
Pentland Rd. HP21: Ayle 1B 12
Perch Mdw. HP22: Halt 1B 22
Peregrine HP19: Ayle 2A 6
Perry La. HP27: Bled 1H 31
Perry St. HP22: Wend 4A 22
Petersfield HP22: Sto M 4E 13
Peters La. HP27: Par H, Whit, Mon R 6H 27
Pevensey Cl. HP21: Ayle 2D 12
Peveril Cl. HP21: Ayle 2D 12
Philips Rd. HP19: Ayle 5E 5
Phipps Cl. HP20: Ayle 3C 6
Picasso Pl. HP19: Ayle 3D 4
Pickenfield OX9: Tha 4F 25
Picts La. HP27: Prin R 4D 32
Pike Cnr. HP21: Ayle 2E 13
Pilgrims Cl. HP27: Mon R 6F 27
Pine St. HP19: Ayle 4D 4
Pink Hill HP27: Par H 5H 33
Pink Rd. HP27: L Grn, Par H 6H 33
Pintail Cl. HP19: Ayle 1A 6
Pipit Gdns. *HP19: Ayle 1A 6*
(off Ayleswater)
Pipit Wlk. HP19: Ayle 1A 6
Pitcher Wlk. *HP19: Ayle 6E 5*
(off Jeffrey Wlk.)
PITCH GREEN 1H 31
Pitt Cl. HP22: Sto M 4E 13
Pitters Piece HP18: Long C 2A 16
Place Farm Way HP27: Mon R 5F 27
Players Theatre, The 3D 24
Playford Ct. OX9: Tha 3D 24
Pleasaunce, The HP22: Ast C 2E 15
Pleck La. OX39: King B 6A 30
Plested Ct. HP22: Sto M 5E 13
Plough Cl. HP21: Ayle 4A 12
Plover, The HP19: Ayle 1A 6
Plover Wlk. *HP19: Ayle 1A 6*
(off Ayleswater)
Plym Cl. HP21: Ayle 2G 11
Poets Chase HP21: Ayle 1B 12
Polish Av. HP22: Halt 1E 23
Popes Acre HP17: Hadd 4F 17
Pope Way HP21: Ayle 3A 12
Poplar Cl. HP20: Ayle 3C 6
Poplar Rd. HP20: Ayle 3C 6
Poplars, The HP22: Wend 4C 22
Poplars Cl. HP17: Sto 2A 10
Poppy Rd. HP27: Prin R 3E 33
Portal Rd. HP22: Halt 3D 22
Portway HP17: Sto 3C 10
Portway Rd. HP17: Sto 2C 10
Pottery Cl. HP19: Ayle 6E 5
Pottery Ct. *HP19: Ayle 6E 5*
(off Pottery Cl.)
Pound St. HP22: Wend 5B 22
Prebendal Av. HP21: Ayle 6G 5
Prebendal Cl. HP20: Ayle 5H 5
Prebendal Ct. HP20: Ayle 5H 5
PREBENDAL FARM 6G 5
Prebendal Ho. *HP20: Ayle 5H 5*
(off Prebendal Cl.)
Prestwold Way HP19: Ayle 6E 5
Prestwood Ho. *HP19: Ayle 6E 5*
(off Prestwold Way)
Priest End OX9: Tha 2C 24
Primrose Ct. *HP21: Ayle 1F 11*
(off Primrose Dr.)
Primrose Dr. HP21: Ayle 1F 11
PRINCES ESTATE 2D 32
PRINCES RISBOROUGH 1F 33
Prince's Rd. HP21: Ayle 5A 6
Princes Risborough Station (Rail) 3D 32
Printers End HP19: Ayle 5F 5
Priory Cl. HP19: Ayle 3G 5
Priory Cres. HP19: Ayle 3G 5
Puffin Way HP19: Ayle 2B 6
Pump La. OX9: Tha 3D 24
Purbeck Cl. HP21: Ayle 2D 12
Pursell Pl. HP27: Prin R 6F 27
Putlowes Dr. HP18: Fleet M 1A 4
Putman Cl. OX9: Tha 3F 25
Putnams Dr. HP22: Ast C 2D 14
Pym Wlk. OX9: Tha 2D 24
Pyncombe Cl. HP27: Prin R 6F 27

Q

Quakers Mead HP22: West T 4H 13
Quakers Mede HP17: Hadd 3G 17
QUARRENDON 3E 5
Quarrendon Av. HP19: Ayle 3F 5
Queens Cl. OX9: Tha 1D 24
Queensgate HP19: Ayle 5E 5
Queens Mead HP21: Ayle 6E 7
Queen's Pk. HP21: Ayle 5B 6
Queens Pk. Arts Cen. 5B 6
Queens Rd. HP27: Prin R 1G 33
OX9: Tha 4E 25
Queen St. HP20: Ayle 5C 6
Quilters Way HP22: Sto M 1F 21

R

Rabans Cl. HP19: Ayle 3C 4
Rabans La. HP19: Ayle 4C 4
Radnor End HP20: Ayle 3A 6
Railway St. HP20: Ayle 5A 6
Rainborough Gdns. HP20: Ayle 3A 6
Rake Way HP21: Ayle 4H 11
Ramworth Way HP21: Ayle 1C 12
Rannal Dr. OX39: Chin 5C 30
Raquets Fitness Cen. 2D 24
Raven Cl. HP19: Ayle 2B 6
Ravensbourne Rd. HP21: Ayle 4H 11
Ravensmead OX39: Chin 5D 30
Read Dr. HP22: Bier 1E 7
Read Ho. *HP19: Ayle 6E 5*
(off Horton Cl.)
Reading Cl. HP19: Ayle 2E 5
Rectory Mdw. OX39: Chin 4D 30
Redcliffe Wlk. HP19: Ayle 3F 5
Reddings Cl. HP22: Wend 3B 22
Red Gallery, The 3D 24
Redland Way HP21: Ayle 2C 12
Red Lion La. HP27: Long 5B 26
Red Wing HP19: Ayle 2A 6
Redwood Dr. HP21: Ayle 6A 6
Reflexions Health & Leisure 2H 5
Regency Ct. HP21: Ayle 6D 6
Regent Rd. HP21: Ayle 6D 6
Rembrandt HP19: Ayle 3D 4
Retreat, The HP27: Prin R 1F 33
Reynold Dr. HP20: Ayle 3C 6
Richmond Rd. HP20: Ayle 5E 7
Rickard Cl. HP21: Ayle 4H 11
Rickford's Hill HP20: Ayle 5H 5
Rickman Wlk. *HP19: Ayle 6E 5*
(off Fairford Leys Way)
Riders Way OX39: Chin 5C 30
Ridge Cl. HP21: Ayle 4H 11
Ridge Way HP18: Long C 4D 16
Ridgeway Ct. *HP20: Ayle 4A 6*
(off Stirling Av.)
Ridgeway Meads HP27: Bled 1H 31
Riley Cl. HP20: Ayle 5G 5
Rimmington Way HP19: Ayle 4F 5
Ringstead Way HP21: Ayle 2B 12
Ripon Ho. HP21: Ayle 1B 12
Ripon St. HP20: Ayle 5H 5
Risborough Rd. HP17: Gt Kim 4A 28
HP17: Lit K, Terr 6A 20
HP22: Sto M, Terr 6D 12
Risborough Swimming & Fitness Cen. 1E 33
Rivets Cl. HP21: Ayle 1A 12
Rixons Mdw. HP19: Ayle 6E 5
Roald Dahl Gallery 5H 5
(in The Buckinhamshire County Mus.)
Roberts Dr. HP19: Ayle 3H 5
Roberts Rd. HP17: Hadd 3G 17
Roberts Way HP21: Ayle 1F 11

38 A-Z Aylesbury

Robin Cl.—Walton Way

Robin Cl. HP19: Ayle 2B 6
Robinson Cl. HP19: Ayle 2D 4
Robins Pl. OX39: Chin 5B 30
Roblin Cl. HP21: Ayle 3A 12
Rochester Pl. HP19: Ayle 5F 5
Roman Way HP19: Ayle 5F 5
Romney Rd. HP21: Ayle 3A 12
Rooks La. OX9: Tha 3D 24
Rose Av. HP19: Ayle 3G 5
Rosebery Rd. HP22: Ast C 2E 15
Rosemary La. HP17: Hadd 2G 17
Rosemead HP22: Halt 6E 15
Rosemoor M. HP19: Ayle 5D 4
Rothesay Cl. HP20: Ayle 4A 6
Rothschild Av. HP22: Ast C 2E 15
Roundhead Dr. OX9: Tha 1D 24
Round Hill HP17: Sto 2B 10
Roundhill Ct. HP17: Hadd 1E 17
Rowan Cl. HP21: Ayle 3A 12
Rowborough Rd. HP22: Halt 2D 22
Rowland Way HP19: Ayle 6F 5
Rowsham Rd. HP22: Bier 1E 7
Roxwell Path *HP20: Ayle 3B 6*
(off Bryanston Av.)
ROYAL BUCKINGHAMSHIRE HOSPITAL, THE 4H 5
Royal Mead HP17: Terr 5E 21
Rubens Cl. HP19: Ayle 3D 4
Rudd's La. HP17: Hadd 2G 17
Run Furrow HP17: Hadd 2G 17
Rupert Way OX9: Tha 2E 25
Rushall Rd. OX9: Tha 2E 25
Ruskin Way HP20: Ayle 3H 5
Russell Av. HP21: Ayle 1G 11
Rutherford Rd. HP21: Ayle 3A 12
Rycote La. OX9: Tha 4A 24
Rye Cl. HP21: Ayle 3H 11

S

St Agnes Ga. HP22: Wend 4A 22
St Andrews Ct. OX9: Tha 3D 24
St Andrew's Rd. OX39: Chin 6C 30
St Andrews Way Ind. Est. HP19: Ayle 4G 5
St Anne's Cl. HP22: Wend 4B 22
St Anne's Rd. HP19: Ayle 5F 5
St Anthony's Cl. HP19: Ayle 5F 5
St Catherine's Ct. HP19: Ayle 5F 5
St Edmund's Cl. HP19: Ayle 5F 5
St Hilda's Ct. HP19: Ayle 5F 5
St James Way HP22: Bier 2D 6
St Johns Dr. HP17: Sto 2A 10
St John's Rd. HP20: Ayle 4A 6
St John's St. HP20: Ayle 4A 6
St Mark's Rd. HP21: Ayle 6G 5
St Mary's Row *HP20: Ayle 5H 5*
(off St Mary's Sq.)
St Mary's Sq. HP20: Ayle 5H 5
St Michaels Cl. HP22: Halt 1C 22
St Peter's Av. HP19: Ayle 2G 5
St Teresas Cl. HP27: Prin R 1F 33
St Tiggywinkles Wildlife Hospital 5H 17
Salisbury Cl. HP27: Prin R 2G 33
Sandhill Way HP19: Ayle 5E 5
Sandpiper HP19: Ayle 1A 6
Sandpit La. HP27: Bled 1H 31
Sandy La. HP18: Long C 3A 16
Saunders Pl. HP19: Ayle 6E 5
SAUNDERTON 5D 32
Savernake Rd. HP19: Ayle 3G 5
Sawmill Rd. HP27: Long 4B 26
Scarlett Av. HP22: Halt 3E 23
School La. HP17: Dint 5H 9
HP18: Che 1C 16
HP22: West T 5G 13
Scott End HP19: Ayle 3D 4
Seaton Dr. HP21: Ayle 3H 11
Sedgemoor Dr. OX9: Tha 2E 25
SEDRUP 3E 11
Sedrup La. HP17: Hart 3D 10
Selkirk Av. HP19: Ayle 3H 5
Selwyn Ct. HP21: Ayle 1D 12
Seven Acres OX9: Tha 3E 25
Sevenacres HP18: Long C 2A 16
Sewell Cl. HP19: Ayle 3D 4
Sewell's La. OX39: Syde 5A 30
Shaftesbury Ho. HP21: Ayle 6E 7
Shakespeare Way HP20: Ayle 5C 6
Shambles, The *OX9: Tha 3D 24*
(off Butter Mkt.)
Sharman Beer Ct. OX9: Tha 3C 24
Sharp Cl. HP21: Ayle 2A 12
Shaw Cl. HP20: Ayle 5C 6
Shaw Ct. HP21: Ayle 4A 12
Sheerstock HP17: Hadd 4E 17
Sheerwater HP19: Ayle 1A 6
Sheffield Dr. HP21: Ayle 1A 12
Shellduck Cl. HP19: Ayle 2A 6
Shepherd Cl. HP20: Ayle 3C 6
Shereway HP19: Ayle 5F 5
Sheridan Cl. HP21: Ayle 4H 11
Sheriff Cl. HP19: Ayle 5F 5
SHOOTACRE CORNER 5E 33
Shootacre La. HP27: Prin R 4D 32
Shortborough Av. HP27: Prin R . . .6F 27
Short Ditch HP17: Hadd 2G 17
Shupp's La. HP18: Che 1C 16
Sidney Ter. HP22: Wend 4B 22
Silverdale Cl. HP20: Ayle 4H 5
Silver St. HP20: Ayle 5H 5
Simmons Ct. HP21: Ayle 3A 12
Simmons Way OX9: Tha 2D 24
Simpson Pl. HP21: Ayle 2B 12
Singleton Way HP19: Ayle 5E 5
Skippon Way OX9: Tha 1D 24
SKITTLE GREEN 1G 31
Skittle Grn. HP27: Bled 1G 31
Slade Hill HP19: Ayle 6E 5
Slattenham Cl. HP19: Ayle 6F 5
Slave Hill HP17: Hadd 4F 17
Smeaton Cl. HP19: Ayle 4D 4
SMOKY ROW 2A 28
Somers Lees HP19: Ayle 5E 5
Somerville Way HP19: Ayle 5F 5
SOUTHCOURT 1G 11
South End HP17: Hadd 4F 17
Southern Rd. HP19: Ayle 4G 5
OX9: Tha 3C 24
Southfield Rd. HP20: Ayle 5D 6
HP27: Prin R 2G 33
South St. HP22: Wend 5B 22
Southwold Cl. HP21: Ayle 1C 12
Sovereign Ct. HP19: Ayle 4H 5
Sparrow Cl. HP19: Ayle 2B 6
SPENCERSGREEN 2H 23
Spenser Rd. HP21: Ayle 1B 12
Spickett's La. HP18: Cudd 4B 8
Spiert, The HP17: Sto 2B 10
Spirit Health & Fitness Club 6F 7
Springfield Cl. HP19: Ayle 5G 5
Springfield Gdns. OX39: Chin 4C 30
Spring Path OX9: Tha 3C 24
Springs Cl. HP17: Elle 1D 28
Springs La. HP17: Elle 6D 20
Spruce Rd. HP19: Ayle 5D 4
Spurt St. HP18: Cudd 4B 8
Square, The HP18: Long C 3A 16
Stablebridge Rd. HP22: Ast C 3F 15
Stable Rd. HP22: Halt 2D 22
Staddle Stones HP27: Prin R 1F 33
Stadium, The 2H 5
Stafford Keep HP19: Ayle 5E 5
Stanbridge Cl. HP17: Hadd 2G 17
Stanbridge Rd. HP17: Hadd 2G 17
Standfield Cl. HP19: Ayle 5E 5
Standring Pl. HP20: Ayle 3B 6
Stanhope Cl. HP22: Wend 2A 22
Stanhope Rd. HP20: Ayle 5C 6
Starling M. HP19: Ayle 5D 4
Stars La. HP17: Dint 5G 9
Station App. HP22: Wend 5B 22
Station Rd. HP17: Lit K 1A 28
HP22: Sto M 6D 12
HP27: Prin R 3E 33
OX39: Chin 4C 30
Station Way HP20: Ayle 5H 5
Station Yd. OX9: Tha 4E 25
Staveley Cl. HP21: Ayle 1F 13
Stephenson Cl. HP19: Ayle 5F 5
Stirling Av. HP20: Ayle 4A 6
Stock Ho. Pas. *HP20: Ayle 5H 5*
(off Market St.)
Stocklake HP20: Ayle 4B 6
Stocklake Ind. Est. HP20: Ayle 4B 6
Stocklake Pk. Ind. Est. HP20: Ayle 4C 6
Stockwell HP17: Hadd 3G 17
Stockwell Furlong HP17: Hadd . . .3G 17
Stockwell La. HP17: Mead 1B 26
Stoke Farm La. HP21: Ayle 4A 12
Stoke Leys Cl. HP21: Ayle 4A 12
STOKE MANDEVILLE 5D 12
STOKE MANDEVILLE HOSPITAL 3B 12
Stoke Mandeville Sports Stadium 3B 12
Stoke Mandeville Station (Rail) 5D 12
Stoke Rd. HP21: Ayle 1A 12
Stokes Cft. HP17: Hadd 3G 17
(not continuous)
Stokes End HP17: Hadd 2G 17
Stokes La. HP17: Hadd 2G 17
STONE 2B 10
Stonebridge Rd. HP19: Ayle 2F 5
Stonechat HP19: Ayle 2A 6
Stone Ct. HP17: Sto 2B 10
Stonehaven Rd. HP19: Ayle 3F 5
Stopps Orchard HP27: Mon R 6G 27
Stork Cl. HP19: Ayle 2B 6
Stour Cl. HP21: Ayle 3G 11
Strafford Way OX9: Tha 3E 25
Stratford Dr. HP21: Ayle 1F 11
Stratfords Way HP17: Hadd 3G 17
Stratton Grn. HP21: Ayle 1D 12
Stratton Path HP21: Ayle 1E 13
Stratton Rd. HP27: Prin R 2E 33
Streamside Wlk. HP21: Ayle 1G 11
Stuart Way OX9: Tha 3E 25
Stubble Hill HP19: Ayle 5E 5
Stuchbury Cl. HP19: Ayle 5E 5
Studland Cl. HP21: Ayle 2D 12
Sulby Cl. HP21: Ayle 2G 11
Summerleys Rd. HP27: Prin R 6C 26
Sunny Brook Cl. HP22: Ast C 1D 14
Sussex Cl. HP19: Ayle 2E 5
Sutherland Wlk. *HP21: Ayle 2B 12*
(off Mellstock Rd.)
Swale Rd. HP21: Ayle 2G 11
Swallow La. HP22: Sto M 5C 12
Swallows La. HP19: Ayle 5D 4
Swan Cl. HP19: Ayle 2B 6
Swan Hill HP18: Cudd 4B 8
Swan M. HP22: Wend 4B 22
Swann Rd. HP22: Halt 1C 22
Swift Cl. HP19: Ayle 2B 6
Sycamore Cl. HP18: Long C 3A 16
Sycamore Ct. *HP19: Ayle 4H 5*
(off Willow Rd.)
Sycamore Dr. OX9: Tha 3B 24

T

Tack La. HP17: Hadd 3F 17
Talbot Rd. HP22: Ast C 2E 15
Tamar Cl. HP21: Ayle 3G 11
Tavistock Wlk. *HP20: Ayle 3A 6*
(off Elmhurst Rd.)
Taylor Rd. HP21: Ayle 2H 11
Tedder Rd. HP22: Halt 4D 22
Tees Rd. HP21: Ayle 2G 11
Telford Cl. HP19: Ayle 4D 4
Templecroft Ter. HP17: Upt 3H 9
Temple Sq. HP20: Ayle 5H 5
Temple St. HP20: Ayle 5H 5
Tennyson Rd. HP21: Ayle 1B 12
TERRICK 5E 21
Terry Dr. HP19: Ayle 2G 5
Thackeray End HP19: Ayle 3D 4
THAME .3D 24
THAME COMMUNITY HOSPITAL 3E 25
Thame Pk. 6E 25
Thame Pk. Bus. Cen. OX9: Tha . . .4E 25
Thame Pk. Rd. OX9: Tha 6D 24
Thame Rd. HP18: Long C 4B 16
HP21: Ayle 6G 5
HP27: Long 4A 26
OX9: Tha 4B 16
OX9: Tow 4H 25
OX39: Chin 2A 30
Thame Rd. Sth. HP19: Ayle 1F 11
Thame Sports & Arts Cen. 3A 24
Thame Tennis Club 3F 25
Thame United FC 4C 24
Thompson Cl. HP21: Ayle 1F 11
Thompson Wlk. *HP21: Ayle 1F 11*
(off Primrose Dr.)
Thorne Way HP20: Ayle 3B 6
HP22: Buck 3G 15
Thorns Cl. HP27: Whit 6A 28
Thorns La. HP27: Whit 5A 28
Thornton Cres. HP22: Wend 4A 22
Thorpe Cl. HP21: Ayle 3C 12
Thrasher Rd. HP21: Ayle 1H 11
Thrush Cl. HP19: Ayle 2B 6
Tibbys La. HP18: Cudd 4B 8
Tichborne OX9: Tha 3E 25
Timber Way OX39: Chin 5C 30
Tindal Rd. HP20: Ayle 3A 6
Tinterne Cl. HP21: Ayle 1E 13
Titmus Rd. HP22: Halt 2E 23
Tiverton Cres. HP19: Ayle 2G 5
Todd Cl. HP21: Ayle 1F 11
Toll Bar Cnr. HP27: Long 4B 26
Tolman Ct. HP21: Ayle 1F 11
Tomkins Cl. HP22: Ast C 3F 15
Tompion Rd. HP19: Ayle 4D 4
Torridge Rd. HP21: Ayle 3H 11
Tourist Info. Cen. Thame 3D 24
Tower Ho. *HP20: Ayle 5A 6*
(off High St.)
TOWERSEY 4H 25
Towersey Dr. OX9: Tha 4F 25
Towersey Rd. OX9: Tha 3F 25
Towersey Way HP21: Ayle 6F 5
(not continuous)
Town Farm Barn HP27: Prin R 2F 33
Town Farm Cl. OX9: Tha 3B 24
TOWNSEND 2G 17
Townsend Piece HP19: Ayle 4G 5
Townside HP17: Hadd 3F 17
Trebah Sq. HP19: Ayle 5D 4
Trenchard Av. HP22: Halt 3D 22
Trenchard St. HP19: Ayle 5E 5
Treves Grn. HP21: Ayle 2A 12
Triangle Bus. Pk. HP22: Sto M . . .1F 21
Tring Hill HP22: Buck 4H 15
HP23: Tring 4H 15
Tring Rd. HP20: Ayle 5D 6
HP21: Ayle 5B 6
HP22: Wend, Halt 5C 22
Trinity Ct. HP19: Ayle 4H 5
Trout Hollow HP27: Saun 5D 32
Tudor Ct. HP20: Ayle 5C 6
Turner Cl. HP20: Ayle 2B 6
Turner's Mdw. HP22: Ast C 1B 14
Turner Wlk. *HP20: Ayle 2B 6*
(off Turner Cl.)
Turnfurlong HP21: Ayle 6B 6
Turnfurlong La. HP21: Ayle 6B 6
(not continuous)
Turnfurlong Row *HP21: Ayle 1C 12*
(off Turnfurlong La.)
Turnham Way HP19: Ayle 6F 5
Turnip Cl. HP18: Che 1C 16
Turnpike End HP21: Ayle 1B 12
Turnstone Way HP19: Ayle 2A 6
Turvey Cl. HP22: Ast C 2E 15
Turville Rd. HP21: Ayle 1F 13
Twitchell La. HP22: Ast C 2E 15
Tyneham Cl. HP21: Ayle 3D 12
Tyne Rd. HP21: Ayle 3H 11

U

Up. Abbotts Hill HP19: Ayle 6E 5
Up. Church St. HP18: Cudd 4B 8
UPPER HARTWELL 2C 10
Up. High St. OX9: Tha 3D 24
Up. Hundreds Way HP20: Ayle 5A 6
Up. Icknield Way
HP22: Ast C, Halt 3C 22
HP27: Bled, Prin R 4G 31
HP27: Whit, Prin R 3F 33
(not continuous)
UPTON 3H 9
Upton Rd. HP17: Dint, Upt 5G 9
Upton Ter. HP17: Upt 3H 9

V

Vale Ho. HP19: Ayle 5G 5
Vale Ind. Cen., The HP19: Ayle 4G 5
Vale Pk. Dr. HP20: Ayle 5A 6
Vale Retail Pk. HP20: Ayle 5A 6
Vale Rd. HP20: Ayle 4A 6
Van Dieman's Rd. OX9: Tha 4D 24
Van Diemens Cl. OX39: Chin 4C 30
Vane Rd. OX9: Tha 3F 25
Verney Wlk. HP21: Ayle 1H 11
Verwood Rd. HP20: Ayle 3A 6
Vicarage Cl. HP22: Wend 4A 22
Vicarage Rd. HP21: Ayle 2H 11
Vickery Cl. HP21: Ayle 2A 12
Vickery Way *HP21: Ayle 2A 12*
(off Vickery Cl.)
Victoria Mead OX9: Tha 4E 25
VICTORIA PARK 5C 6
Victoria St. HP20: Ayle 5B 6
Victory Rd. HP22: Wend 4B 22
Villiers Bldgs. *HP20: Ayle 5H 5*
(off Buckingham St.)
Vincent Rd. HP19: Ayle 2E 5
Vinetrees HP22: Wend 5B 22
Vineyards, The HP27: Bled 1G 31
Viney La. HP19: Ayle 5D 4
Viscount Cl. HP20: Ayle 3B 6

W

Waddesdon Grn. *HP21: Ayle 4A 12*
(off Winterton Dr.)
Wainwrights HP18: Long C 3B 16
Waivers Way HP21: Ayle 3C 12
Walker Dr. OX9: Tha 4F 25
Walkers Rd. HP27: Long 4B 26
Wallace End HP21: Ayle 1C 12
Wallbridge Cl. HP19: Ayle 6F 5
Walnut Cl. HP18: Long C 2A 16
HP22: Sto M 5E 13
Walnut Cres. HP27: Long 4B 26
Walnut Dr. HP22: Wend 3B 22
Walnut Tree Ct. HP22: Sto M 4E 13
Walnut Tree La. HP27: Long 5B 26
WALTON COURT 2G 11
Walton Ct. Cen. HP21: Ayle 2G 11
Walton Dene HP21: Ayle 6B 6
WALTON GREEN 6A 6
Walton Gro. HP21: Ayle 6A 6
Walton Pl. HP22: West T 4H 13
Walton St. HP20: Ayle 5H 5
HP21: Ayle 6A 6
Walton Way HP21: Ayle 6C 6

A-Z Aylesbury 39

Y